Self Effectiveness
The Power of Meditation

Self Effectiveness
The Power of Meditation

S. K. Palhan

> *Dedicated to my wife*
> **Dr. Santosh Palhan**

STERLING PAPERBACKS
An imprint of
Sterling Publishers (P) Ltd.
Regd. Office: A1/256 Safdarjung Enclave,
New Delhi-110029. CIN: U22110DL1964PTC211907
Tel: 26387070, 26386209; Fax: 91-11-26383788
E-mail: mail@sterlingpublishers.com
www.sterlingpublishers.com

Self-Effectiveness: The Power of Meditation
© 2016, Prof. S. K. Palhan
ISBN 978 93 85913 81 5

All rights are reserved.
No part of this publication may be reproduced, stored in a retrieval system or transmitted, in any form or by any means, mechanical, photocopying, recording or otherwise, without prior written permission of the author.

Printed in India

Printed and Published by Sterling Publishers Pvt. Ltd., Plot No. 13, Ecotech-III, Greater Noida - 201306, Uttar Pradesh, India

Contents

	Acknowledgements	vi
	Introduction	1
1.	Self-Effectiveness	7
2.	The Infinite Potential of Human Beings	15
3.	Mind and Its Wandering	21
4.	Self-Effectiveness through Meditation	35
5.	Benefits of Meditation	51
6.	What Else Can Make People More Effective?	61
7.	Types of Meditation	83
8.	Scientific Studies on Effectiveness of Different Types of Meditations	87
9.	Conclusion	99
	Appendix 1: Vedantic Understanding of Mind	102
	Appendix 2: Brief on Different Types of Meditations	110
	Glossary	158
	References	161

Acknowledgements

I am grateful to His Holiness Jagadguru Shankaracharya Bharati Teertha of Sringeri for his guidance in pursuit of self-development and giving an opportunity to introduce the practice of meditation for self-effectiveness to management students in Sringeri Sharada Institute of Management (SRISIM). I wish to express my deep gratitude to Swami Parmananda Bharati for teaching me the fundamentals of Vedanta on the banks of Ganga and inspiring the need of values in our professional and personal life, and Swami Someshwarananda for introducing the fundamentals of meditation to me and my students in SRISIM in 1996.

I sincerely thank the following persons and organizations who have played important role in evolution of this book:

- R. K. Palhan, CEO, Delhi School of Yoga, my elder brother, for his inspiration and dedication to spread the practice of yoga and meditation in a large scale in the Indian railways, which reduced the accidents due to human errors.
- Mohan Lakhamraju, Vice Chairman of Great Lakes Institute of Management, for giving me freedom to teach self-effectiveness besides the conventional teaching to professionals undergoing management education.
- Sunil Kumar, for editing the book, with his vast knowledge and also the help in understanding the broader concept of mind in Vedanta.
- Lt. General (Retd.) H. S. Lidder, a role model for a visionary and effective leadership, for giving valuable inputs for the chapter on what else can make persons more effective.
- Late Mr. K. S. Bhutoria, Chairman of Pathfinder Trust, for providing an opportunity to understand the Jain philosophy and Prekshadhyan meditation.
- Fore School of Management, Bharatiya Vidya Bhawan, National Institute of Financial Management, Institute of Applied Manpower Research and Delhi Judicial Academy for giving me opportunities for introducing the concept of self-effectiveness in their programmes.

Prof. S. K. Palhan

Introduction

Human beings have infinite potential. There are a few people who have been highly effective and they have left a mark on the history of mankind. Human beings are engaged in different activities to achieve their goals. Highly effective people may leave their mark in terms of ideas, products, services or institutions. They are recognized for the implementation of their ideas which have changed the world. There are many scientists, but few Edisons or Einsteins. There have been millions of businessmen, but few like Henry Ford, George Welsh, Dhirubhai Ambani and J. R. D. Tata. There have been many philosophers but few like Jesus, Krishna, Prophet Mohammad, Buddha, Adi Shankaracharya, Guru Nanak, Swami Vivekananda, Aristotle and Plato. There have been many sportsmen, but few like Pele, Maradona, Dhyan Chand, Brian Laura, Nadia Comaneci and Sachin Tendulkar. Observe any field, be it science, humanities, sports, or any other and you will find that a few people have been highly effective through their outstanding contribution in their field of specialization.

The purpose of this book is to understand some common traits which have made people highly effective in their area of work. Effectiveness comes through action, that is, work done. For performing any work or action, you need suitable skills. The society today is highly skill and information oriented. But if skills were the only criteria for effectiveness, then the most highly skilled people would be the most effective persons. However, it has been observed that the most highly effective people may have only average level of skills.

Some people achieve happiness in life with limited knowledge, skills and resources. In contrast, there are many people who have not achieved their goals in spite of large resources, skills, and knowledge. This book explores the domain of mind to seek the secret of highly effective people.

If we analyze any activity, we will observe that every action is done in two stages. The first is the creation of the action or work in the mind and the second is the physical manifestation of the work. For doing any work, the mind must be available for its creation first. **The nature of the mind is to wander into the past and future, but the action lies in the present moment only.** If the mind is focused on the present moment of time, then it is available for the creation of any action.

Highly effective people are essentially creative people and for this purpose their mind remains in the present moment for action. Effective people have their mind focused on the present moment. It is not diverted from the issues at hand or the present moment. Focus of mind is important for creative solutions of problems. One of the major issues in determining the effectiveness is the ability to keep the mind in the present moment.

The structured method to develop the focus of the mind is meditation. It is also called the sadhana or control (of the mind).

There are many methods of meditation developed by the leading philosophies of the world, e.g., Hinduism or Vedanta, Buddhism, Jainism, Zen Buddhism, Christianity, Sikhism, Muslim and Maya. It is very difficult to identify the best method of meditation because any method is effective provided it suits you and you are able to practise it regularly with the correct technique. In the classical sense, the best option is to learn from an established master or Guru. Some of the methods have been discussed in this book in Chapter 7. See also Appendix 2.

Modern thinkers with a scientific approach look for research to evaluate the effect of meditation on physical and mental capabilities. A lot of research has been done in this direction by many institutions all over the world. The contributions of AIIMS in India and the Heart Math Group in Colorado, USA, are noteworthy. It has been seen that persons who do regular meditation are less prone to stress since they have trained their mind to live in the present moment.

The importance of meditation has been realized by many leading companies of the world. A large numbers of software companies expose their creative people to meditation. It is estimated that more than ten million persons practise meditation in USA.

Meditation is one of the most systematic and structured methods to increase the focus of the mind. However, many people have demonstrated high effectiveness in their lives without the formal practice of meditation. In this book, I have made an attempt to identify some other factors which could enhance effectiveness. Some of these are: self-discipline, keen interest in the work, challenging situation, concentrating on one activity at a time, control over desires, clarity of goals, Satsang (company of good thoughts, and good people), selfless service, discovering the Divine miracle within, and tapping the power of the subconscious mind.

John Spencer has presented the importance of living in the present moment for effectiveness very well in his book, *The Present*. Similarly, Eckhart Tolle has elaborated the same in his book, *The Power of Now*. This book elaborates the factors which keep the mind away from the present moment and the techniques which can help to live in the present. The structured techniques of meditation from different systems have been explained. The book also explains techniques other than meditation which can also help in enhancing effectiveness.

The prevalent education system does not address the mind but emphasises mainly the knowledge and skills. The examination of curricula of the leading universities of the world reveals this. You may examine the curricula of MIT,

Stanford or IITs and IIMs in India. The mind has not been the subject matter of study in the normal academic curricula.

The structured method to control or develop the mind is meditation. It is also called sadhana or control of the mind. Meditation is important for the mind and the body. It has been developed in almost all the philosophies of the world, for example, Vedanta, Jain, Buddhism, Zen Buddhism, Sikhism, etc.

The importance of meditation has been realized by many leading companies of the world, particularly by the companies developing computer software. There are many methods of meditation and the beauty is that virtually all the methods are effective, provided they suit you and you are able to practice them in the correct manner.

This book also describes a few techniques of sadhana, which are easy to learn and yet effective in their purpose. Self-effectiveness is only the visible result of meditation; the invisible but far reaching benefits are in terms of happiness and a better quality of life. What makes a few people highly effective in life compared to others? Is effectiveness due to material resources, knowledge, and skill? This book is an attempt to understand the mystery behind self-effectiveness.

We may observe that some people are highly effective in their life without practicing the classical techniques of meditation. This book also cover some other factors like memory, keen interest, challenging jobs, concentration, control over desires, perseverance, and clarity of goals, which lead to self-effectiveness.

Some of the words in Sanskrit or Hindi language (written in *italics*) are difficult to translate into English and are therefore explained in the Glossary.

Yesterday is history,
Tomorrow is a mystery,
Today is a gift.
That is why we call it the PRESENT!

Babatunde Olatuni

Summary

- Effectiveness is through action and work done.
- Every action is done twice:
    - The first creation of the task is in the mind.
    - The second creation of the task is its physical implementation.
- The creation of task in the mind precedes physical action.
- Skills and energy are important for performing any task effectively and efficiently.
- Managers usually focus on efficiency, but leaders focus on effectiveness through the first creation in the mind
- Skills are important for doing any work. But higher skills alone do not make a person more effective.
- The skill levels of most of the highly effective people are similar to normal persons.
- Work or action can be done only in the present moment of time:
    - Neither in the past
    - Nor the future.
- The mind should be in the present moment for the first creation.
- Effectiveness comes through the utilization of the present moment.

CHAPTER-1

Self-Effectiveness

1. Effectiveness comes from actions

To start with, let us try to understand what we mean by effectiveness. Effective people leave a mark by their work or by implementation of their ideas. Even if you have the best ideas in your mind and you do not implement them, you don't become effective. Bill Gates is effective in Information Technology because of the organization he has created. Sachin Tendulkar was an effective batsman on account of his performances. Mahatma Gandhi is remembered as a highly effective leader due to the freedom he achieved for the nation by his philosophy of non-violence. Similarly, J. R. D. Tata and Dhirubhai Ambani were effective leaders and entrepreneurs because of the organizations they set up.

Mere thoughts do not make a person effective. For example, a person may have an idea of building a monument more beautiful than the Taj Mahal or Eiffel Tower, but he will be recognized only if he implements his ideas. Effective leaders are characterized by the implementation of their lofty vision. Vision comes through the thought process. Effectiveness comes through the implementation of thoughts through action and work done.

The first creation of the work in the mind is an individual phenomenon, but implementation may require energy group effort and teamwork, where leadership plays a very important role. Highly effective persons are invariably very good leaders also. The focus of this book is on self-effectiveness.

2. First creation of the task is in the mind

Since effectiveness is characterized by work and action done, let us examine further as to how work and action is done. Observe a tennis player hitting a ball. He has the option to hit the ball through a forehand or a backhand stroke. The return stroke is made by the hand, but does the hand decide which way to play the ball? The hand obviously does not have the power to decide the type of return stroke. The return stroke is decided in the mind. Let us call the decision in the mind as the **first creation** of the stroke. After the first creation of the task in the mind, the skills of the player come into action to execute the stroke physically.

Let us take another example of a simple activity of switching off a computer. Even when we have the skill and capability to switch off a computer, we will do it only when the first creation of task, that is, switching off the computer, comes in the mind.

3. Effectiveness needs skills

In both these examples, the action may look as an instantaneous response, but the fact is that every physical action is preceded by its first creation in the mind. Therefore, every task is done in two steps. The first creation of any task is in the mind and the second creation is the physical manifestation of the task. The physical implementation of a task requires suitable skills. For example, if you want to cook food, you should have the appropriate skills to cook. For communication in a particular language, you must have the skill of that language. You cannot weld two components unless you have the skill of welding. Therefore, skills are important for the physical execution of any task.

The main stress of education and training institutions is in building of a variety of skills like reading, writing, mathematics, sciences, technology, accounting, cooking, cycling, playing, singing, painting, etc. This is required because even a simple work or action cannot be done without

Self-Effectiveness

adequate skills. For the selection of suitable manpower for any job, adequate skills are a prerequisite.

4. Work is done in the present moment of time

Let us examine the time dimension of work, that is, the time when the action or work can be done. Experience shows that work can be done in the "present moment of time". Even the most powerful people cannot go back in time to perform an action. For example, if the time now is 11 a.m. on November 29, then it is not possible to perform an action at 10.45 a.m. on November 29, or the day before or the previous week. Time which is past is gone for ever and no action is possible at a time which has already passed the present moment and gone into the past.

We can plan to do a work in the future, but when the work is being executed, it would be, again, the present time. It is not possible to move forward to perform an action in future time.

Therefore, work is possible in the small window of time, which opens in the present moment. His Holiness Dalai Lama defines the present moment as 1/360th of the time taken for a *chutki*. This concept can be better understood through the following diagram:

		FUTURE

Time ⟶

Present Moment (The Window for Action)

The flow of time is along the X-axis, from the left to the right side. The blue represents the past, i.e., time which has already passed. The green represents the future time that has yet to come. In between the past and the future is the window of the present moment where all the action takes place. This small window represents the present moment and moves along the X axis. For doing any task, the mind should be in the present moment to enable first creation of the task. If the mind is in the past, it would not be available for first creation of the task. And unless there is first creation, the physical manifestation of the task cannot take place. To perceive the opportunity for action, the awareness of the mind should be in the present moment. Similarly, when the mind wanders to the future, as in the case of a day dreamer, the mind is not available for the first creation and the opportunity in the present moment for action is missed. This would reduce the effectiveness of the person.

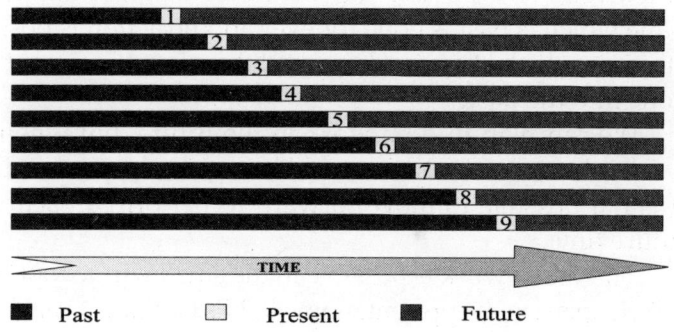

This diagram shows the flow of the "present moment" from window number 1 to 9 along the X axis. If we are in window 3 of the time frame, then it is not possible to perform any action in window 1 and 2, but we can plan for action in windows 5 or 6. When we are actually in window 2, we can plan for the activities in windows 3, 4, 5 and 6. Suppose we plan for an activity in window 6, then though the planning may be done at the window 2, the action leading to effectiveness will be performed only when we reach window 6 (if done at that time).

Awareness precedes choice which precedes results.
Robin Sharma

Success is no accident (big idea). And it's easy to forget that successful people didn't start that way. They started off as ordinary persons — with a dream, a plan and goals.

Then they made daily 1% improvements. The days slipped into weeks, the weeks slipped into months and the months slipped into years. Their dream grew and became real. Yet the first, and most powerful step, took place in their minds.

5. Role of skills in effectiveness

5.1

As mentioned earlier, the stress of the present day education and training is on building the various skills like reading, writing, communicating, computing, management, etc. This view is supported if you examine the subjects taught at the leading academic institutions in the world like MIT and Stanford in USA, Oxford and Cambridge in UK, or IITs and IIMs in India. This is necessary because skills are important for performing any action. Even the simple activity of picking up a pen from the table by hand requires skill of eye-hand coordination. This complexity can be appreciated only when you try to program a robot to do the same job. In the process of industrial and technological development, the variety of skills required has grown in width as well as depth, e.g., programing was one skill earlier, but today you have variety of skill sets like various programing languages, vectors ,graphics, etc., representing different skills in programing.

5.2

There is a general assumption that skills make a person more effective in executing a task. Let us examine this assumption in the light of our past experience. One of the measures of skill level or proficiency in a subject is the marks or grades given by an evaluation mechanism. The evaluation implies that higher the marks or a grade in an examination, higher is the skill level in that subject. In actual practice, it is observed that the persons who have higher level of skills (supported by higher marks or grades) may not be more effective compared to the persons who have lower grades or skill level. If you plot the percentage of marks received by your classmates and their effectiveness in life, normally you may expect that higher the marks, higher should be the effectiveness (as shown in Fig. A). But actual experience has shown that the situation represented in Fig. B to be the reality. Thus we see that there is hardly any correlation between skill level and effectiveness in life.

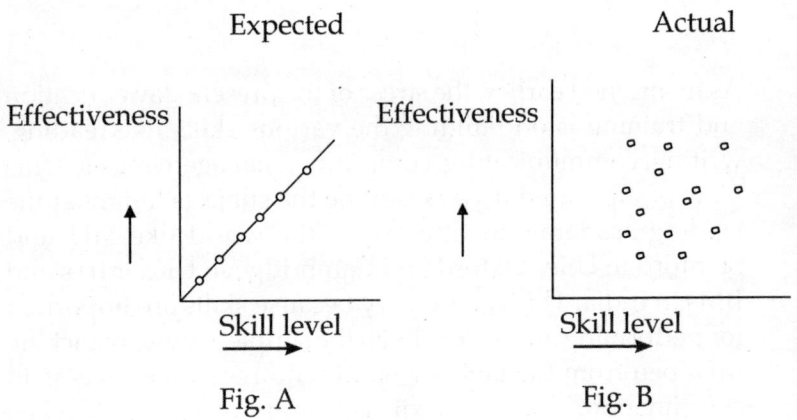

Fig. A   Fig. B

5.3

Let us look at the skill sets of some of the people who are highly effective in their lives like Bill Gates, Sachin Tendulkar, J. R. D. Tata, and Dhirubhai Ambani. If you examine the skill sets of Bill Gates, who did not have a formal university education, his skill sets in the I.T. area are fairly good, but there are many people in his company whose skill sets are much higher than his. Bill Gates admitted this during his visit to India in 2002 and said that many Indians had I.T. skills better than him. On a rough estimate, there are more than 76,000 software engineers in India whose skill sets are equal or more than Bill Gates, but none of them are as effective as him.

5.4

Let us look at the second example of Sachin Tendulkar as an effective batsman. The skill sets for a good batsman are footwork, ability to play a variety of balls, power to hit and run ability to see the ball, etc., in different formats of the game. There are dozens of players whose skills as a batsman are comparable to that of Sachin Tendulkar, but none of them is as effective as him.

5.5

Take the third example of two of the most effective entrepreneurs or businessmen in India, namely, J. R. D. Tata and Dhirubhai Ambani. Both of them had average skills and many of their employees had better skill sets than them, but none of the employee could be as effective as them. If skills alone were the criteria for effectiveness, then teachers of management would have been the most effective managers.

5.6

You may look at your own circle of friends. Estimate their skill levels based on their academic performance and their relative effectiveness in life, and plot that on a scatter diagram as shown in Fig. B. You will observe that effective people have average skill sets and there is little correlation between skill levels and effectiveness. By and large, skilled people are more efficient in their work but not necessarily more effective. In this context it may be observed that good managers are characterized by good skill sets and efficiency in work. But leaders are different from managers and their focus is on effectiveness, whereas the managers focus on efficiency.

Summary

- Human beings have infinite potential.
- Effective persons are able to make the best use of their potential in the present moment, where the action is.
- Ordinary humans waste their potential by
    - Worrying about the past,
    - Undue anxiety about the future,
    - Emotional disturbance and
    - Undirected activities, other than on the task at hand in the present moment.

CHAPTER-2

The Infinite Potential of Human Beings

1.

*H*uman beings have infinite potential. This statement is supported by virtually all the leading philosophies of the world. In the *Vedantic* philosophy, one of the important statements is *Aham Brahmasmi*, i.e., I am *Brahma* (*Brahma* is the creator of the universe according to *Vedantic* philosophy). In Bible it is stated that "God created man in His own image" and we know that the potential of God is infinite. Thus, the human potential is compared to that of *Brahma*, who created this entire universe. Now if the human potential is infinite, why only a few effective persons are able to harness the infinite potential and the bulk of the people are not able to utilize their potential? We know that the most effective people are neither cast in a different mould nor do they have skills higher than others.

2.

Therefore the question arises: If the effective people have ordinary skill sets, then what makes them different from ordinary people? Let us go back to the earlier discussion on effectiveness. People are effective on account of the action or work done, and every action is done twice—first creation is in the mind and the second creation is through skill sets.

If the skill sets of effective people are ordinary, then the extraordinary effectiveness come from the first creation, and **the first creation of any work takes place in the mind**. Therefore, let us examine the operation of the mind.

3.

The natural tendency of the mind is to wander to the past or the future. It is estimated that an average person entertains more than 65,000 thoughts in a day. The mind goes to the past when we are thinking of past events. Similarly, the mind may go to future, that is, think about the future with anxiety. The anxiety may be on various issues, for example, passing an examination, getting promotion or getting married to the right person. Sometimes, the mind may get the anxious about the state of the investment in future. Now, when the mind has drifted to the past or future, it is not available in the present moment for first creation. When the first creation is not possible due to the absence of the mind from the present moment, the second creation is not possible. Without the second creation of the task, effectiveness cannot happen. Thus effectiveness is reduced or absent when the wanders into the past or future.

4.

In addition to past worries and activities about the future, the mind may be affected by emotional disturbances also. Even a highly skilled person loses his effectiveness when he is emotionally disturbed due to some grief, fear or anger. People lose their creativity when they are emotionally disturbed. Many people have the habit of thinking repeatedly about the past events, which brings emotional disturbance. A single event in the past can go on nagging at the present moment and reduce effectiveness. The mind carries the load of unpleasant events from the past for long and makes a person ineffective in the present moment, since the mind can only dwell either in the present or the past at the same time.

5.

Take the example of a middle-aged lady who was mentally disturbed frequently because of the remarks made by her mother-in-law 20 years ago. She was haunted by the past events all the time. When the mental disturbance became too much, she consulted an expert. During the diagnosis it emerged that her mother-in-law had rebuked her on an issue about 20 years ago and this episode played again and again in the mind of the lady since that time. The expert suggested that she should forget the incident and enjoy her normal life. The interesting issue in this case was that the mother-in-law had died 3 years earlier, but the memory of the event still made her angry every time. Many of us carry the grudges of the past on our shoulders which keeps the mind mentally disturbed. In Jain philosophy, a lot of importance is given to the act of forgiveness. They celebrate a specific day every year when you seek forgiveness for your mistakes and also forgive others. In the northern parts of India, people celebrate the festival of Holi, in which you are supposed to forget the past grudges and forgive others.

6.

The issue is: can we forget an unpleasant event of the past or should we go on deepening its memory by revising it again and again? The mind denies the present habitually but this habit can be broken. Many of us do not take advantage of the present moment and let the mind live almost exclusively through the memory of the past and anxiety about the future. This keeps the mind preoccupied with the past and the future and there is no opportunity to have the full potential of the mind for the first creation of an activity or for implementation in the present moment. Such persons miss all the opportunities for action in the present moment.

When the mind goes to the past, it leads to worries and when the mind goes to future it leads to anxiety. In between the past and the future is the narrow window of the present moment that leads to effectiveness. When the mind is full of problems of the past and anxieties of the future, then where is the room for utilization of full potential for creative action to solve or enjoy the present moment? The scope for creativity and action lies only in the present moment.

7.

Someone may argue that if we forget the past, then how we would learn from the experience since experience comes from the past only. The answer is simple — learn from the past, but do not keep thinking of the past. If the unpleasant thoughts from the past invade the mind, show no interest and do not entertain them. Let the mind observe the unpleasant thoughts and let them pass. Dwelling on the past is like replaying a bad movie again and again and getting disturbed by it. Suppose, you are driving a car and your eyes are focused on the rear view mirror most of the time. If you do this, you lose the perspective of the present moment that is immediately before you. You may look at the rear view mirror when you are changing your lane or stopping suddenly. But you cannot drive safely looking at the rear view all the time!

8.

Similarly, another argument may be that we must plan for our future and how can we do that if we are keeping the mind in the present moment. There is a fallacy in this argument also. When is the future planning done? It is done in the present moment only! The problem is not with planning for the future but with living mentally in the future. When I am planning a summer holiday, I am examining the future options now, but if am mentally stuck on the chosen destination and continue thinking about it all the time, and miss the opportunity to buy the tickets in time, then where is the action based on the planning? Thus, we must distinguish between planning for the future in the present moment as against day dreaming about the future in the present moment. We should remember that the action of learning from the past or planning for the future is essentially done in the present moment only.

To summarize the issue, we must learn from the past, plan for the future, but live in the present moment for effectiveness.

The Indian philosophy on this subject is summed up in a wise saying:

Gate shoko na kartvyo bhavishyam na chintayate
Vartmaan kaalen vilakshnam
Chanakya Neeti Chapter 13.2

(One should not to grieve for the past nor worry for the future. Wise care for the present and chart their course accordingly.)

And this sums up the theme of this book also.

Human beings have a choice. The plant and animal kingdoms have very little choice. Their behaviour is programmed by their instinctive nature. If a cow is hungry, it will eat the grass offered to it. It will not exercise any choice. Human beings have a choice — a patient or a priest may decide not to eat even when he is hungry. Human beings are not dictated by instinct alone. We can exercise the choice for the mind to remain in the present moment instead of in the past or the future.

Summary

- The mind is a flow of thoughts.
- Functions of the mind:
    - *Manas:* instruments for perception through senses
    - *Chitta:* mind stuff; storehouse of memories, experiences and perceptions
    - *Budhi:* intellect to take decisions
    - *Ahankaar:* identification with self
- Characteristics of the mind:
    - Gets input through the five senses; Fluctuating and difficult to control; Driven by likes and dislikes; Negative thoughts make it weak; Every thought, word and deed leaves an impression on the mind; A weak mind succumbs to temptations, creating pain and misery
    - Vedantic view of the mind and universal mind is given in Appendix 1.
    - Management of mind is through: Self-discipline
- Live in the present moment: That is where the action is, to lead you towards self-effectiveness and bliss.
- Though all human being have infinite potential, the potential for first creation in the present moment is reduced due to various factors like: Past worries ,Future anxiety , Emotional disturbance and Undirected activities

Chapter-3

Mind and Its Wandering

1. The mind and its functions

The mind can be understood as a flowing river of thoughts. The mind is a field for all feelings, emotions, and thoughts. It is the coordinating instrument for perception and actions. It is the storehouse of all memories, which continuously build and reconstruct our beliefs, values, likes and dislikes, tendencies, and worldview. Human beings continuously interact with the external world. The mind is the only instrument of perception and the field where all sense data that we continuously receive through the sense organs gets sorted out, processed, decisions taken, and instructions given to organs of action to act. The mind is "one," but performs four functions and performs them at a lightning speed, so that we do not see the process.

i) *Manas*: Whatever we hear, feel, see, taste, or smell from external sources comes into us from the sense organs and *manas* perform the function of coordinating the input data. It does not know what the data represents, it just receives it.

ii) *Chitta*: The data received through the sense organs and coordinated by the manas is then referred to the *chitta*, the stuff, or field of mind. Chitta functions as the memory bank. All that we have ever thought, spoken, or done leaves an impression (*samskaras*) on our chitta.

iii) *Buddhi*: The new, raw data along with the comparative data stored in the chitta is then presented to the *buddhi* (intellect). Buddhi then performs the function of determining and deciding. Buddhi can decide wrongly or correctly based on previous data in chitta.

Buddhi has to be trained and awakened, through continuous practise, to choose and act correctly. This practise creates new and better *samskaras* or impressions in the chitta. This refined buddhi is *Viveka*, which can decide and choose *right*. Right is defined as that choice which will enable us to go towards the higher dimensions of work and life, towards the source of consciousness, a state of consistent success, happiness, peace, and bliss, and our common universal goal.

Vivek-buddhi helps our growth towards perfection. The dynamic power of Buddhi is *will*, the desire, determination, and power to do the right thing. Vivek needs to be awakened through continuous practise of self-development efforts, like fulfilment of duties, sincere striving for quality and perfection in whatever we do, care and concern for others, working for the good of all, righteous conduct, etc., supported by regular prayers, meditation, worship, etc., according to our respective traditions.

iv) *Ahamkara*: *Ahamkara* is the function of the mind which appropriates the data to myself, and leads to the I-sense like I am doing, etc. The eyes see something. The Manas receives and sends the data to Chitta. Chitta looks into memory bank of stored comparative data and sends it to buddhi, which decides—a cow is running. Ahamkara says the cow will hurt me.

2. We are what our mind is

All out thoughts and desires arise from tendencies we have acquired and are acquiring every moment by our present thoughts-actions. We are identified by our mind and our desires. What we desire, we resolve to do; as is our resolution, so is our action. And whatever we carry out into action that we reap. The mind, by nature, flows towards pleasures, temptations, and towards what we have enjoyed in the past. To change our mind-set and force it to go towards the higher dimensions is very difficult; it needs life-long practise and focus on the higher goals. We have to train our mind to take us every moment towards the highest perfection. For all practical purposes, we can say that we are what our mind is. The mind is built to enable us to perceive the external world. In a way it can be considered as a villain because it restricts our understanding based on our own past thoughts and actions. It loves to look outside for satisfaction and prevents us from identifying with the life, consciousness, and atman, which are our real self and our inherent nature.

3. Characteristics of the mind

The mind imbibes that on which it dwells and it prefers to dwell on what it likes. The mind wants enjoyment. *I* want success. The mind will not give up easily. Only repeated better thoughts and repeated better habits can overcome past tendencies and impressions. There is no short cut—practice and detachment is the only way. The mind keeps going either to trivia or its likes and dislikes. From trivia, we have to learn to withdraw through *abhyasa (practice)*. From likes and dislikes, we have to learn to detach through withdrawal from lower levels and focus on the higher levels. This is *vairagya* or detachment.

Both wanted and unwanted thoughts flow through the mind. We can observe these thoughts. Thus, we are the subject as well as the observer of the mind at the same time. We are not the thoughts; we are the knower. We usually forget this and get identified with our thoughts and flow with them.

Every thought, word, and deed leaves an impression on our mind. Depending on our attachments, we get bound by these impressions. We are often slaves of our impressions, which can be considered of three types: *sattvic* (calm and virtuous, leading to higher dimensions), *rajasic* (action oriented, passionate), and *tamasic* (not alert or attentive, suitable for routine). The *tamasic* mind has to grow through *rajas* towards the *sattvic* mind.

Just as a bottle of ink is cleaned by pouring fresh water into it, in the same way we can clean the mind by pouring better thoughts and inculcating better deeds. This may be done by reading better books, speaking better words, keeping better company, and by doing better deeds.

Negative and evil thoughts, words, and deeds make the mind weak. A weak and uncontrolled mind always succumbs to temptations, creating pain and misery. Brooding over past failures gives rise to negative thoughts.

4. Managing the mind

By its very nature, the mind is restless like a monkey and therefore very difficult to control! The more the control you have over your mind, the greater a person you are. The mind has a tendency to flow down — be tempted to enjoy the experiences of the senses. It gets attached easily, but detaches with difficulty. Awareness that "I am not the mind" helps in control. Continuous, regular, repetitive practice is needed to purify and develop the ability to manage the mind.

Mind management is really Thought Management. We have to manage the ever rebellious mind like a Mother (with love), Father (discipline with love), Teacher (strict do's and don'ts), Unwanted Guest (just ignore), and Police (forcefully ensure compliance). Continuous exposure to good thoughts is the best method of giving a new direction to the flow of thoughts.

Through practise, we have to develop the habit of becoming aware of the flow of thoughts in the mind. Flow of thoughts has three aspects to be managed: Quantity, Quality and Direction.

i) Quantity: Higher the frequency and number of thoughts that is, quantity, the more is the mind disturbed. Thoughts are a load on the mind. Do not carry the load of unwanted thoughts. Learn how to stop creating unwanted thoughts. Following a timetable and keeping busy with planned activities is the best method for keeping the quantity of thoughts under check.

ii) **Quality:** Pour good thoughts into the mind to remove unwanted thoughts. The remedy is thinking about positive, strength giving thoughts — the infinite strength that is already within.

Fulfilling our duties, striving for quality in whatever we do, and care and concern for others also leads to *chitta-suddhi*. Quality of thoughts can also be improved by the company of value based persons, reading good books, and performing prayers. As we think, so we become; therefore be very careful of the thoughts you entertain, the company you keep, and the books you read.

Always aim for the highest and the best. Manifesting the infinite potential within, this will enable you to meet your short-term goals also.

iii) **Direction:** The mind is one-track in nature. It is very difficult to change the direction of thoughts. By entertaining the opposite thoughts, we can gradually strive to change the track. When angry or hateful, think of love and goodwill, think of the divinity. Continuous exposure to good thoughts is the best method of giving a new direction to the flow of thoughts

5. Actions for managing our mind

Make a resolution to lead a disciplined life. Practice watching the flow of thoughts in your mind, as an unconcerned witness. As you practise, you learn to recognize the coming in of unwanted thoughts. You can start managing and throwing out the unwanted thoughts. Once you resolve to be disciplined you start fighting the unwanted thoughts. Awareness that you are not the thoughts, recognizing that you do not need to follow the unwanted thoughts, is the first step. Prayers, *Shraddha* and humility are of great help.

Do not be a slave to your thoughts. Be the master. Fix a routine, set up a time table for your life. Practice adhering to your routine. It may be difficult in the beginning, but keep on trying. Never mind the failures. Gradually learn to control your mind. Discipline and time table forces the mind to become our slave.

There are many difficulties in mind-management. Some factors which make it difficult to manage our mind are: Not fulfilling our duties to society, organization, or self; not striving for quality and Improvements in work; not leading a value based life; strong likes and dislikes (attachments and aversions); habit of deliberately hurting or harming others; indulging in intoxicants, living an unbalanced and undisciplined life; habit of fault-finding and gossip; becoming over-ambitious, jealous, self-righteous, egocentric, etc.

6. Mind in *Vedanta*

The mind is discussed in great detail in the *Upanishads* and *Vedanta*. The concept of mind is also linked to the creation of the universe. A brief about this is given in Appendix 1 at the end of this book.

6.1

The mind also has the option to wander away from the present and it does this remarkably well. A normal mind may entertain more than 60,000 thoughts in a day. A large number of them may be repetitive. When we are in the office, the mind can wander to the problems or issues at home. Alternately, we may be having dinner at home, but the mind may be tackling the issues of the office. Thus, when we are actively engaged in an activity, the mind may flit to another activity. This is the nature of mind and this cuts down the potential to act on the activity or job at hand in the present moment. The concept of the present moment can be understood best through the diagram discussed earlier in Chapter 2.

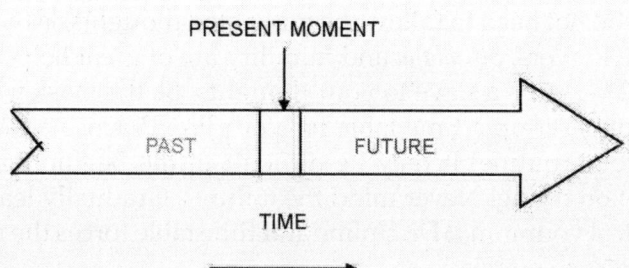

The time is flowing along the x-axis (in one direction only) as shown by the arrow. The blue part represents the past that is, time which has already passed and the green part represents the future time, that is, the time which is yet to come. In between the past and the future is the window of the "present" moment. This window of the present moment represents the flow of time from left to right in the diagram. Action is possible only in the present moment of time. Though human potential is infinite, but its utilization varies widely. Let us examine the factors that reduce the functions of the mind for action in the present moment.

6.2

When the mind goes to past, it is engaged mentally on the activities which happened in the past. For example, a cricket player may be mentally worried about what happened in the previous series of matches. If his mind is busy in viewing the past, then it is preoccupied with the past moments and it is *not* available for first creation for any activity in the present moment. The mind being in the present moment means that the mind is available to perceive the incoming ball (the present moment) if he is batting. The player may lose his wicket if the mind is not in the present moment to perceive the incoming ball. And unless there is first creation of the action to be taken (e.g., hitting on the offside on back foot), the body will not be able to perform the stroke. In this situation, all the skills learnt are of virtually no use because the skills to perform an action come into action only after the first creation of the task has been done in the mind. In such a case mind may suggest alternate actions (or strokes) in the given situation and the final decision is taken by the intellect (*buddhi*). The steps in the playing of a ball could be analyzed as follows:

i) Mind in the present moment to focus the eyes on the incoming ball (the present moment) through the sensory perception of eyes.

ii) The mind interprets the motion of the incoming ball (e.g., an in swinger or a full toss) and generates following

alternates to tackle the ball, based on the habits created in the past and recorded in the chitta:
- Defensive stroke
- Off the back foot
- Hit on the mid onside
- Cut it on the offside
- Hit on the long on.

iii) The intellect function of the mind decides which stroke to play (based on the developed skills).

iv) The "I" sense function of the mind makes the body react to execute the stroke (act) in the present moment. This action requires skills for the coordination the ball, eye, foot, hand, and bat to execute the stroke. This is based on habits created in the past and recorded in the chitta (memory part of the mind).

It may be observed from this example that the mind has a very key role in playing the ball before the action takes place by the body. The important thing to understand here is that, every time, the entire potential of the mind should be on the incoming ball. And the moment the mind slips into the past (e.g., a squabble with the captain or the selection committee) or future (e.g., how he will enjoy the shopping with the family after the match), the effectiveness to execute the stroke would be lost.

6.3

Sometimes, the mind may be emotionally disturbed (and this would also come from the past, e.g., the person may be in anger or sorrow). When the mind is reacting emotionally to the memory of the past in the present moment, then also the mind is not available to perceive the incoming ball (the present moment). This would also reduce the potential of the mind to act.

Mind and Its Wandering

6.4

One more factor can reduce the effectiveness of the mind to act in the present moment. Imagine a group of young children in an arithmetic classroom, looking at the black board while a teacher is explaining the method of subtraction. The teacher is very strict and, therefore, all the children are concentrating at the black board. One of the windows of the classroom is open and a few children are flying a kite in the adjacent lawn. Though the eyes of the children are towards the blackboard, their minds are focused on the movements of the kite in the sky. Can the children be effective in learning the subtraction technique being taught on the black board? In this case, the activity on the black board and the flying of the kite are taking place in the present moment, but if the purpose at that moment was to learn, then the mind is pursuing undirected activities. When the mind is not directed or focused towards the activity at hand and it goes to some other activity, then this also reduces the effectiveness of the current activity.

6.5

The above behaviour is not restricted to children — most of us indulge in it. We are often engaged in many projects or tasks at the same time. When we are at task X, the mind goes to issue in Y or Z and when we are doing task Y, the mind may go to task X and Z. Thus the mind may not be in the present moment, where the action is awaiting. We tend to spend a lot of time in thinking about activities other than the task at hand. This process can be summed up as the mind getting engaged in undirected activities.

Whenever the mind dwells on the past events or future activities, it can lead to major disasters, such as in the case of a train driver who ignores a red signal because of his preoccupation with the past events or activities at home. The driver is required to be alert and vigilant in the present moment at that time and avoid major disasters resulting in loss of lives and property.

6.6

To summarize, the potential of the mind for first creation in the present moment is reduced when the mind:
i) Goes to the past, ii) Goes to the future, iii) Gets emotionally disturbed, or iv) Gets engaged in undirected activities.

All the above four avenues reduce the availability of the mind for the first creation of the task at hand. This can be seen through the following diagrams:

The above diagrams are not to scale, but drawn to understand the various components that reduce effectiveness of the mind. In actual practice, the phenomenon is highly dramatic and it cannot be understood unless you have experienced in your own mind. The four factors may take different values at different times, but the net effect is the reduction in effectiveness.

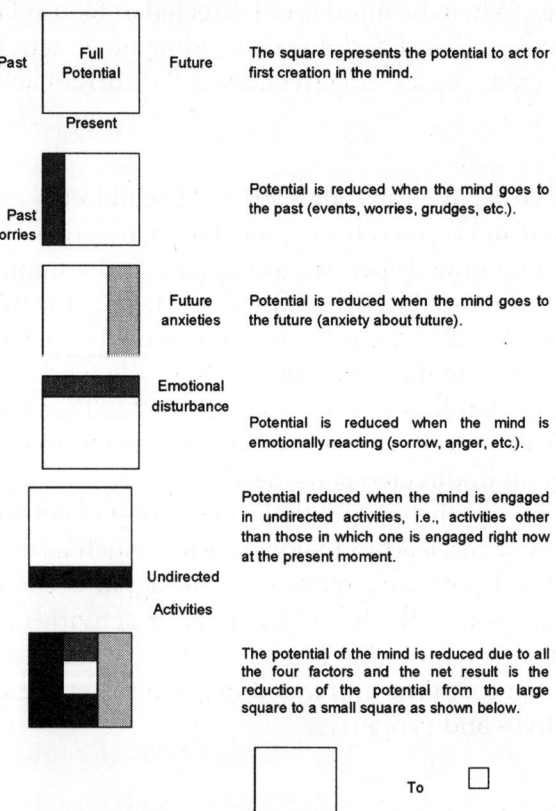

7. Focus the mind

Please read the following paragraph carefully and then do an exercise on self-introspection of your mind. **This exercise is very important before you go ahead with the book.**

- Sit comfortably on a chair, feet on the ground, back straight, i.e., the head, neck and vertebral column in a straight line, but relaxed.
- Kept the hands free on your lap.
- Close your eyes gently.
- Try to become aware of your national flag for about 60 seconds.
  - The colours should be sharp and true.
  - Imagine the flag stationery, no fluttering.
  - No poles or hoisting ropes.
  - Choose any background and keep it fixed.
  - Be aware of the flag only and nothing else.

After 60 seconds open your eyes gently and record what you saw in the last 60 seconds, when the eyes were closed. Use the space given below:

```
                                                    
                                                    
                                                    
                                                    
```

You will realize that in most of the cases we are not able to focus on the flag alone and there are many other things also which we think. Some may find it difficult keep the flag stationery. This above exercise gives you an experience of the way with which your mind operates. We are not able to keep the mind focused even for just a minute on an object.

I have repeated similar exercises with a variety of persons, for example, managers, students, housewives, unskilled and skilled workers, and highly skilled software engineers. The results are similar and most of the people are not able to focus their mind on the object selected even for short period of 60 seconds. The impact of this statement can be appreciated only if you actually experience your own mind.

In actual life, when the eyes are open, the diversions for the mind become more prominent. Most of the tasks that we do are not of such a small duration as one minute. We may take five minutes to write a short email and one hour to write an official report. We may need a few hours to plan for an important event and it may take a few years when we are engaged in building an organization. Now, when the duration of an activity becomes longer, the ability to keep the mind focused on it becomes more difficult. When the mind is not focused on the task or the job at hand, it is not available for first creation of any important activity and when there is no first creation in the mind, physical manifestation of the activity cannot take place. In this situation, the potential of the mind is utilized to a very small extent. In ordinary human beings, the potential is reduced dramatically as shown in the following diagrams:

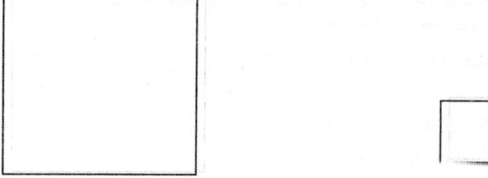

Potential of mind   Utilization of potential of mind

The ability to focus the mind in the present moment increases the utilization of potential for first creation of any activity in the mind. The stages of effectiveness may be seen as:

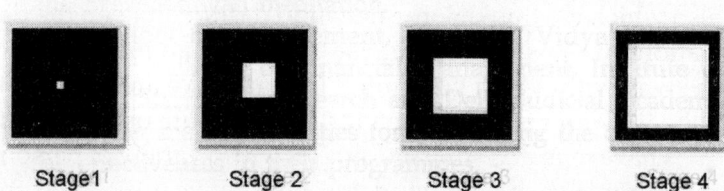

Stage 1   Stage 2   Stage 3   Stage 4

Mind and Its Wandering

Between Stage 1 and 4, the difference is not of a small percentage, but it can be a few hundred or thousand times. This represents the difference between an ordinary person and a highly effective person. Even with ordinary skill levels, highly effective people are more effective due to a far superior focus of mind for the first creation of any work or task.

You can experience this in your daily life also. The activity may be:
- Cooking a meal • Listening • Reading a book
- Driving a car • Attending a lecture on a new subject
- Creative work like painting, wood carving, etc.
- Identifying the cause of a problem • Doing your project work

Whenever you do your work with the full involvement of the mind in the work, you are more effective in terms of output as well as the quality of output. Your skills remain the same, but you are far more effective when your mind is fully engaged on the work at hand.

- "Awareness precedes choice which precedes results."
- Success is no accident (big idea). And it's easy to forget that successful people didn't start that way. They started off as ordinary persons—with a dream, a plan, and goals. Then they made 1 per cent improvement every day. The days turned into weeks, the weeks into months, and the months into years. Their dream grew and became real. Yet the first and most powerful step took place in their minds

Robin Sharma

Let him who would enjoy a good future waste none of his present.

Roger Babson

Summary

Meditation is the structured method to live in the present moment. It can be learnt. It leads to self-effectiveness, reduces stress and anxiety, and improves the quality of life in all dimensions. It improves:
- Relaxation of the mind
- Physical health
- Creativity
- Self-development and spirituality

Chapter-4

Self-Effectiveness Through Meditation

The mind is a flow of thoughts. The mind is controlled by likes and dislikes. *Vairagya* gives the freedom to the mind. Some of the practices which are recommended to control the mind are *yama, niyama, asanas, pranayam, pratyahar, dharma, dhyan, and samadhi*. Detailed explanation of these terms is given in Chapter 7. These practices help in the process of increasing self-effectiveness.

Meditation keeps the mind relaxed in the present moment. The mental stress rarely comes from the task at hand in the present moment. It usually comes from the worries about the past or anxieties about the future. Many people live mentally in the past and review their worries and grudges frequently. This leads to mental stress. Some people may revisit mentally the events that took place in the past. They scratch their wounds of the past and do not allow them to heal. The past events may have little relevance today, but if you are worried about them, then this also leads to stress.

Similarly, some persons are under anxiety about the future all the time. Every step that they take, they have anxiety about the next step and this does not allow them to make most of the present moment, where the action is. Over-anxiety about the future can be a major source of tension in the mind. Some students who are preparing for examinations are under so much anxiety that they are not able to concentrate on their present activity. In the meditation process, we try to keep the mind fully engaged in the present moment. We try to ensure that the past worries and future anxieties are not entertained by the mind. To increase effectiveness, the mind should learn to remain in the present moment and focus on the job at hand. This aspect of self-development or self-effectiveness is not touched in the conventional education system in India or anywhere else at present. The best structured system for focusing the mind is meditation. Meditation can be done through a variety of techniques and the beauty is that virtually all techniques are effective. The various techniques may seem to be totally different from one another, but the essence of all the techniques is same.

The first result of meditation is the clarity of mind and improved ability to focus. Ordinary sunlight becomes very powerful when it is focused through a lens. A laser beam is a highly focused and coherent beam of light, which can cut through tough materials. Meditation provides access to the unlimited potential of the mind.

Effectiveness is usually referred to as *siddhi* in Indian philosophy and it is considered as a result of meditation or *Sadhana*. The higher benefits of meditation are self-development in physical, mental, and spiritual dimensions. For the present, we are trying to understand only the limited benefit for effectiveness.

Indian literature is full of instances where people acquired great powers and exhibited very high effectiveness in different fields or situations. Let me share with you an experience of mine. In 1996, I had the opportunity to become the Founder Director of Sri Sringeri Sharada Institute of Management at New Delhi. The Institute was set up with the blessings of H. H. Jagadguru Shankaracharaya of Sringeri. It was a management school with a difference. It planned to conduct post-graduate management programme (PGDBM), equivalent to MBA, based on the Indian value system and the modern management techniques. As a part of the Indian system, meditation was an integral part of the education. In a new management institute, we were only able to attract students with mediocre skill levels as judged through the traditional examination system.

After six months of the commencement of the course, we sent a team of 3 students to participate in a management game competition conducted by the All India Management Association at New Delhi. There were 23 teams from well-established companies and management institute. The management game was simulation of running a business in a highly competitive environment. All the teams were given equal virtual capital to start the business. All the teams were required to take a large number of decisions, e.g., investment in production capacity, R&D, training, pricing, and marketing in order to optimize the profit. A computer simulated the market results, based on which each team had to prepare their Profit and Loss account as well as the balance sheet.

The game continued for 2 days and simulated operations of 10 years. It required a great deal of mental focus on the variables in the game. Surprisingly, our team stood second in 23 teams in spite of the fact that all the other 22 competitors had higher skill levels. The strategic advantage our team had was the capability to focus, since they had been doing meditation regularly. Some people thought that it was by chance, but the views changed when a new team repeated a similar performance next year.

The meditation technique taught to the students had been developed after discussion with large number of experts. Often, some meditation techniques are very complex and some have a large number of restrictions, which are difficult to fulfil. The technique taught to the management students was easy to learn and practise, even in a common office environment. The details of the technique are as follows:

Meditation Process

Preparation:
- What to do?

    Choose a suitable method of meditation? All methods are effective provided they suit you and you practice it regularly

- When to do?

    Morning, evening; fixed or variable time and duration
- How to do?

    Self-learning, learning from a guru
- Where to do?

    Location inside or outside, fixed or variable, on ground or on chair.

Criteria for choice

- Less chance of disturbance
- Fresh air
- Can fit into your daily schedule
- Don't worry too much about the duration and quality of meditation. It is more important to just do it regularly.

After a bath, wear clothes which are loose and comfortable for the weather conditions.

- Take your seat and the posture.
- Keep your back straight and hands in a comfortable position.
- Close your eyes gently, with eyeballs directed downwards.
- Take in a long breath and exhale it gently, chanting OM. The mouth is open when you utter O, and the mouth is closed automatically while uttering M in OM.
- Repeat this above process of inhaling deeply and exhaling while chanting OM three times.
- Be aware of your environment and listen to the variety of sounds all around you (for about 2 minutes).
- Be aware of your body from head to the toes and remember that:

- you are not the Body
- you are not the Mind
- you are not the Intellect
- you are not the Ego
- you are a part of HIM
- Be aware of your body parts one by one for one breathing cycle as follows:
  - be aware of your head
  - be aware of your neck
  - be aware of your shoulder
  - be aware of your arms
  - be aware of your chest
  - be aware of your abdomen
  - be aware of your thighs
  - be aware of your legs
  - be aware of your feet
  - be aware of your toes
- Be aware of your total face—face—face—
- Be aware of your left ear—left ear—left ear—
- Be aware of your right ear—right ear—right ear—
- Be aware of your left cheek—left cheek—left cheek—
- Be aware of your right cheek—right cheek—right cheek—
- Be aware of your left eye—left eye—left eye—
- Be aware of your right eye—right eye—right eye—
- Be aware of your chin—chin—chin—
- Be aware of your forehead—forehead—forehead—
- Be aware of your lips—lips—lips—

- Now be aware of your breath. Observe your inhaling and exhaling. Breathing shall be normal (you may observe the breath near the nostrils). This may be done for 3 to 4 minutes. If the mind wanders, then take a deep breath and bring the awareness of the mind back to the breathing process. The most effective breathing is at the rate of 10 to 12 cycles per minute.
- To complete the process, say OM while breathing out gently and then rub the palms of the hands vigorously and then touch both the palms on the eye lids and then open the eyes gently.

Note: Do not worry about the time taken for meditation. It may take 7 to 10 minutes. More important is to do it regularly.

J. Krishnamurti defines meditation in a different way. He says:
1. A meditative mind is silent. It is not the silence which thought can conceive of; it is not the silence of a still evening; it is the silence when thought—with all its images, its words, and perceptions—has entirely ceased. This meditative mind is the religious mind—the religion that is not touched by the church, temple, or chants.
2. Meditation is one of the greatest arts in life—perhaps the greatest and one cannot possibly learn it from anybody. That is the beauty of it. It has no technique and therefore no authority. When you learn about yourself, watch yourself, watch the way you walk, how you eat, what you say, the gossip, the hate, the jealousy. If you are aware of all that in yourself, without any choice, that is part of meditation.
3. Meditation is a state of mind which looks at everything with complete attention, totally, not just parts of it.

John Kabat Zinn, the author of *Full Catastrophe Living*, has identified seven different attitudes which help to live in the present moment:
1. Non judging
2. Patience

3. Beginner's mind
4. Trust
5. Non striving
6. Acceptance
7. Letting go

These seven attitudes are interrelated and they reinforce one another.

1. Non judging attitude means being an unbiased and attentive witness of the experience in the present moment. If you have very strong likes and dislikes, then your observation may be biased. For example, a person may say, "I don't like citrus fruits," based on his past experience and does not want taste them even when they are good, or a person may say, "I don't like rivers," because he had seen a friend falling into a river. In such cases, the evaluation of the event or things becomes biased.

   The view of Indian ethos on this issue is illustrated in *Drig Dishya Vivek*, which teaches the philosophy that we should learn to be an observer of the events around us. Once you become judgmental of the events and the environment, you are not truly able to live in the present moment.

2. Patience means the ability to bear difficult situations with calmness. Patience comes through self control. Impatient persons are in a hurry to move from one moment to the next moment. For example, students are eager to move from their present class to the next senior class.

3. Beginner's mind — a beginner is like a child who observes everything with wonder. And if you don't have a beginner's mind, then you take things for granted and don't observe the novelty in a situation. You tend to compare it with past experiences all the time and lose the charm of the present moment. A person with a beginner's mind observes every event with an open mind and is able to get involved in the activity in the present moment.

4. Trust—you must trust in yourself and in your ability to develop your mind. If you are in doubt all the time, then the process of meditation would become difficult.
5. Non striving acceptance—We are greatly influenced by our like and dislikes. We want more of the things and situations we like and less of the things we don't like. In this process, we make lot of efforts to change others. When we are trying to change everything around us, then we are striving all the time and not truly living in the present moment. Persons who are not content with the things as they are want to change them and when they are not able to change them, it leads to dissatisfaction.
6. Acceptance allows you to observe the present moment exactly as it is and not as it should be according to your likes and dislikes. An attitude of acceptance allows you to take action. Some people are not able to accept themselves, for example, their short height or dark complexion. This leads to wanting to change the situation and not able to see the beauty of the present situation. Their observations become biased when they observe a person with short height or a dark complexion. They spend a huge amount of their energy and attention to change things leading to tension, instead of making best use of the situation.

    In this context the Indian thought about action is summed up in Gita as follows:

    "You have the right to action but not on its result or outcome." If the result is not to your liking, you should not be disheartened.
7. Letting go—when you are strongly attached to a thing or an issue, it becomes difficult to perceive the present moment truly. Letting go means you reduce your attachment to likes and dislikes. When you let go, you are mentally relaxed and you can be in the present moment.
    - Anxiety and fear is commonly experienced by all persons, irrespective of their health, wealth, and intelligence. Anxiety and fear may come from work, home or, more commonly, from our inner thought process.

- We tend to ignore fear and anxiety like a pigeon who chooses to close its eyes when a cat is attacking it.
- Dr. John Kabat Zin of University of Massachusetts (Medical school) has conducted several studies on panic and anxiety disorder patients and found that meditation (which he refers to as MBSR, i.e., Mindful Based Stress Reduction) benefits the patients.
- *The Relaxation & Stress Reduction Workbook* by Martha Davis, Elizabeth Robbins Eshelman and Mathew Mckay (New Harbinger Publications) describes the following meditation techniques:
  - Mantra meditation
  - Releasing muscular tension through the exploration or body scan
  - Mindfulness and present-moment: Awareness #
  - Mindfulness of pain or discomfort
  - Letting go of thoughts

This includes eating, walking, seeing meditation, visualization technique, which may be receptive, programmed or guided.

Do not allow the clock and the calendar to blind us to the fact that each moment of life is a miracle and mystery."

H. G. Wells

Our emotions are powerful motivators and they drive our behaviour more than almost anything else in our lives. Sometimes, our greatest challenge is to get inside our own heads to understand what makes us feel and behave the way we do. Highly motivated, positive people are focused. Their mind is clear and energy levels are high.

Many things can hold you back and prevent you from becoming all you can be. One of these things is emotional baggage.

I know two family members who were best friends, but several years ago, one reminded the other of something that had happened 30 years earlier. One thing led to another and they haven't spoken since.

Anger or resentment is like a cancer. When you let it go untreated, it will put an invisible ceiling on your future. You don't know it, but it does.

William Ward identified the cure when he said, "Forgiveness is the key that unlocks the handcuffs of hate." These are powerful words and I know from experience that forgiveness works. I've been greatly wronged and taken advantage of a few times in my life. My first reaction each time, of course, was anger and resentment. I held these feelings for a while and felt my stomach tie up in knots, my appetite wane and the joy slip out of my life. The quote from Ward provided the wake-up call I needed to forgive the persons who had wronged me. It was like I had been playing the first half of a basketball game with three-pound steel shoes and in the locker room the coach said, "Try these new shoes in the second half." Multiply that by ten and you'll understand how great it feels to unload your "emotional baggage" through the power of forgiveness.

Forgiveness

When you hold resentment toward another, you are bound to that person or condition by an emotional link that is stronger than steel. Forgiveness is the only way to dissolve that link and get free.

Catherine Ponder

When a member of the Babemba tribe of South Africa acts irresponsibly or unjustly, all work stops. Everyone gathers in the centre of the village and forms a large circle around the offender. Every member of the tribe, regardless of age, shares all the offender's positive attributes, strengths, good deeds, and acts of kindness throughout his or her lifetime which they can recall.

When everyone has recounted all they can remember, the circle is broken and the person is symbolically and literally welcomed back into the tribe with joyful celebration.

Here's *your* math homework—subtract your judgments and blame, add more love and appreciation, and multiply that by your sincerity. It's a sum that can change a person, a village, and the world!

Meditation Techniques

There are many techniques of meditation and some of the popular ones are:
- Transcendental
- Trataka-Candle gazing
- Yoga Nidra-Visualization
- Vipassana
- Preksha dhyan
- Japa
- Pooja rituals
- Beads
- Mantras
- Coherent breathing

The modalities of some of the well known techniques are also given in the *Appendix 2*.

The common element in virtually all the techniques is learning to keep the mind in the present, say, by watching the breathing process. The mind is trained to be aware of the breathing in and breathing out process. You cannot be aware of the breath, which you took five minutes ago, or the breath you are yet to take in the future. Thus, if you are aware of your breath, then mentally you are engaged in an activity which is essentially in the present moment of time. When your mind is in the present moment, you are fully relaxed because the mind is not worried over the past events or the anxiety of the future. The metabolic rate goes down in most of the meditation techniques and the electrical waves in the brain makes it reach a state of relaxation like deep sleep.

In the awakened stage, the mind is flitting all the time between the past, present, and future, leading to emotional disturbance and chaos in the autonomous nervous system. This reduces the ability of the mind to focus on the task at hand and, hence, self-effectiveness. If meditation is practised regularly, then the mind gets into the discipline of remaining in the present moment. This training of the mind helps in improved focus on the activity at hand. With clarity and focus of mind, it is easier to understand any new information, subject, or opportunity. Opportunities, in the shape of problems, come to all human beings, but ordinary people are worried about the past result of the problem and develop anxiety for the future. Instead of worrying about the past and anxiety about the future, the person whose mind is focussed in the present is able to see the problem and convert it into an opportunity. The assumption here is that most of us have adequate skills to perform our activities and what we lack is the ability to focus the mind on the present moment. Meditation gives us the desired edge of clear thinking and ability to act in the present moment for effectiveness.

Impact of Meditation

Let us look at the impact of regular meditation on different aspects of life. If physical exercise of muscles is done regularly, then the muscles develop over a period of time and when an opportunity come to make use of the muscles, you can do it easily.

A mother tells her young son that he will become strong like a hero if he exercises regularly, drinks milk, and take nourishing food. The child exercises for two days and gets disillusioned because the muscles have not grown like the famous hero's! The muscles grow only through constant practice and focus on the right means, i.e., exercise and right food, taken regularly over a period of time. In the case of disciplining of the mind, similar is constant practice and focus is required. It may take a long time and it is not the result of a one-time activity.

Many people give up the practice of meditation because it did not produce the desired miracle of effectiveness. We have allowed our mind to wander in all directions for the last so many years and should not expect it to become disciplined in a few days or weeks. Therefore the result of meditation comes only after regular and proper practice over a period of time, though some people are able to learn the practice earlier. Most of the people give up meditation because they expect results overnight, whereas the art of meditation is a lifelong practise. There is no doubt that highly effective persons have learnt the art of focusing somehow or the other. This is because it is the very nature of the mind to get focused on whatever we like and are attracted towards. So, if we can somehow get a burning desire to succeed, then it becomes easier for the mind to follow.

Effects of Meditation

Let us look at the effect of meditation on different aspects of life:
I   Meditation and relaxation of the mind
II Meditation and physical health
III Meditation, self-development and spirituality
IV Meditation and creativity

I. Meditation and relaxation of the mind

The major cause of disturbances in the mind are worries associated with past events (I did not get good results; my boss rebuked me, etc.). The anxiety for the future is another cause (Will I pass the exams? Will I be accepted in the new job? Will I be able to marry the person I like?). These disturbances keep the mind agitated. Its performance in the present moment is reduced because the mind is not available for the awareness and perception of the present moment. The work itself usually does not give disturbance.

In most of the cases, we get tired from the mental activity of disturbance rather than the physical activity of the work. Mental relaxation is associated with activities in which you are fully engrossed and enjoying the activity. Complete idleness can give you relaxation for a very short time only. Longer stretches of idleness invariably lead to boredom, which is not relaxation. The mind is relaxed when it is fully involved in the activity at hand in the present moment. This may be achieved when the mind has learnt to live in the present moment. The process of meditation keeps your mental awareness in the present moment, thereby excluding

the worries of the past and anxieties of the future. Most of the persons who meditate regularly feel relaxed:
- During the meditation
- Immediately after the meditation
- In the normal course of life

II. Meditation and physical health

It is well known that when faced with a problem, the human response is to flight or fight. In the case of flight, the blood rushes to the spot of physical activity, thereby depriving other vital organs from nourishment for that moment. If we are mentally disturbed most of the time, the first physical effect is on the digestive system. In case of chronic stress conditions, stomach problems, like poor digestion, start and sometimes result in ulcers. In case the food eaten is not digested properly, the physical health is affected immediately. There is very close correlation between the mind and the body. The Heart Math Institute in California has studied, in depth, the effect of worry, anxiety, and negative thoughts on the working of the heart.

III. Meditation, self-development and spirituality

The primary purpose of meditation has always been self-development in various dimensions. In Indian philosophy, meditation is one of the most important steps in spiritual development. All the spiritual gurus like Buddha and Mahavira did extensive meditation for their spiritual growth and ultimate enlightenment.

The smaller objective of meditation is to develop focus of the mind for performing tasks. The task may be a war, governance, or any work requiring technical skills. The meditation process improves the capability to harness the skills to achieve effectiveness. This aspect of meditation has been referred to as *siddhi* in the Indian philosophy. It is considered a low level of achievement if your process stops only here.

When you strive for a higher goal, the lower goals are also automatically fulfilled. So, we can ask ourselves, should we not strive for the higher goals of meditation? If we do so, then effectiveness in studies, work, and relationship will definitely come to us. Moreover, we will ensure that we remain on the critical path to the highest goals also. However, if we try for only a lower goal, then we may perhaps totally miss the higher goal of life.

Physical, mental, and psychic powers are enhanced a lot in a *siddha* person. The integrated development of human personality has the following dimensions: physical, mental, social and spiritual.

The most effective personalities who have left a mark in the history of civilization were the spiritually evolved persons. The ultimate objective of life is happiness and bliss and this needs a meditative mind.

IV. Meditation and creativity

In 1890, at the 25th anniversary of the discovery of the structure of benzene, Friedrich August Kekulé, a German chemist, reminisced about his major accomplishments and talked of two dreams that he had at key moments of his work. In his first dream, in 1865, he saw atoms dance around and link to one another. He awakened and immediately began to sketch what he had seen in his dream. Later, Kekulé had another dream, in which he saw atoms dance around, then form themselves into strings, moving about in a snake-like fashion. This vision continued until the snake-like string of atoms formed itself into an image of a snake eating its own tail. This dream gave Kekulé the idea of the cyclic structure of benzene.

Creative arts like poetry, painting, and designing happen in a relaxed mind. Even the creative strategy of war calls for a relaxed mind.

Summary

Meditation is one of the structured method which leads to self-effectiveness. There are more than one hundred benefits of meditation under the following categories:
- Physiological
- Psychological
- Spiritual

Chapter-5

Benefits of Meditation Practices

*R*egular practise of meditation has multiple advantages. It improves the quality of mind. Meditation makes the mind calm and improves its perception and communication skills. It gives you physical and mental relaxation and inner peace.

Meditation which was limited to the eastern countries has become popular in the west also. Many people adopt it to reduce the stress of modern life and personal growth. The medical science has also realized the benefits of meditation in psychotherapy. In the corporate world, especially the software companies this has become popular for enhancing creativity through calm mind.

Benefits of meditation, based on scientific studies

Over 350 research studies have been conducted on meditation at more than 250 universities and medical schools (including Harvard, UCLA, and Stanford). These studies have been published and peer-reviewed in more than 100 scientific journals. In India also, research has been carried out on the effects of meditation.

http://Wikipedia.org/wiki/research-on-meditation

Scientific studies on impact of meditation

Scientific studies have conclusively proved the benefits of meditation for our mind and body. According to research results released by the University of Wisconsin-Madison,

meditation has been shown to produce lasting beneficial changes in immune-system function as well as brain electrical activity. "Researchers found about 50 per cent more electrical activity in the left frontal regions of the brains of the meditators. Other research has showed that part of the brain is associated with positive emotions and anxiety reduction."
http://www.medicalnewstoday.com/article/272833.php

Research on the effects of different types of meditation has been done by the following organizations in the west:

- Mehmet Oz, M.D., Emmy Award-winning host of The Dr. Oz Show
- National Institute of Health USA
- The American Journal of Cardiology and the American Association of Hypertension and Strokes
- Journal of Psychiatry
- American Journal of Hypertension
- Military Medicine
- Journal of Counseling and Development
- Psychosomatic Medicine
- Alcoholism Treatment Quarterly
- Journal Of Clinical Psychology
- Cedar-Sinai Medical Centre Los Angeles
- UCLA Medical School
- National Institute Of Health in Bethesda, Maryland
- University of California at Irvine
- Mind Body Medical Institute affiliated to Harvard University and Boston hospitals
- Harvard Medical School
- Yale, Harvard, Massachusetts General Hospitals
- Heart Math Institute

In India, research on meditation has been carried out at many institutions like AIIMS and Gangaram Hospital, New Delhi. The details of this are given in Appendix 2.

Development of meditation

Meditation is not necessarily a religious practice, but because of its spiritual element it forms an integral part of most religions. And even though the basic objective of most meditation styles remain the same—performed in a state of inner and outer stillness—they all vary according to the specific religious framework within which they are placed. Preparation, posture, length of period of meditation, particular verbal or visual elements—all contribute to the various forms of meditation. Some of the more popular methods are Transcendental Meditation, yoga nidra, vipassana and mindfulness meditation.

http://www.mindandlife.org

It was not till the 20th century that a need for the creation of secular forms of popular meditative techniques began to be felt. But for the most part these New Age meditative systems were little more than rehashed versions of older techniques, which had been extracted from their religious contexts. Transcendental Meditation (TM), as propagated by Maharishi Mahesh Yogi, is one such version, which grew out of the Hindu practice of naam japa or yog jap during the 1960s.

> There are many schools and styles of meditation within Hinduism. Yoga is generally done to prepare one for meditation, and meditation is done to realize union of one's self, one's atman, with the omnipresent and non-dual Brahman. This experience is referred to as moksha by Hindus, and is similar to the concept of Nirvana in Buddhism. The earliest clear references to meditation in Hindu literature are in the middle Upanishads and the Mahabharata, which includes the Bhagavad Gita.

Within Patañjali's ashtanga yoga practice there are eight limbs leading to kaivalya "aloneness". These are ethical discipline (yamas), rules (niyamas), physical postures (āsanas), breath control (prānāyama), withdrawal from the senses (pratyāhāra), one-pointedness of mind (dhāraṇā), meditation (dhyāna), and finally samādhi, which is often described as the realization of the identity of the Self (ātman) with the omnipresent (Brahman), and is the ultimate aim of all Hindu yogis.
http://Wikipedia.org/wiki/research-on-meditation

Meditation in Hinduism is practised in different forms by different schools and sects and has expanded beyond Hinduism in the West.

The influential modern proponent of Hinduism who first introduced Eastern philosophy to the West in the late 19th century, Swami Vivekananda, describes meditation as follows: Meditation has been laid stress upon by all religions. The meditative state of mind is declared by the Yogis to be the highest state in which the mind exists. When the mind is studying the external object, it gets identified with it, loses itself. To use the simile of the old Indian philosopher: the soul of man is like a piece of crystal, but it takes the colour of whatever is near it. Whatever the soul touches, it has to take its colour. That is the difficulty. That constitutes the bondage.
http://www.medicalnewstoday.com/articles/272833.php

Benefits of meditation

When we start practicing meditation, we start feeling relaxed, peaceful and happy. This is a kind of inter-generative process. You meditate and you get the reward in forms of joy and happiness, which in turn motivates you to meditate more. In course of time, it becomes your automatic practice. You feel uneasy and think something is missing from your life if you do not meditate on any particular day. When you start your day with meditation, the peace and joy generated last with you whole day whatever the nature of your activities. It is like taking a healthy and nourishing diet before the start of a strenuous and stressful routine of the day.

Meditation enables you to become aware of your inner resources of joy and peace. You can tap them whenever you feel stressed and worried. You acquire a habit of detached observation. So if something wrong and irritating happens in course of your day, you can view it as a detached observer. You learn to understand the monkey tricks of your mind. You thus get an inner poise that ultimately percolates into your daily life. The peace and joy that you acquire become infectious to those around you. In this way you try to make the whole environment happy and peaceful.

http://liveanddare.com/benefits-of-meditation

- All meditation practices (almost all) are effective if done properly. Many people learn different techniques but do not practise them regularly and then they claim that they are not getting any benefit! Remember that physical muscles can be developed through regular exercises, but they don't develop after pumping iron dumbbells for just a day. Regular physical exercise is required for the growth of physical muscles. People buy the best of gym equipment, but keep it under lock without using it and then complain that they are not effective. The mental muscles to keep the mind in the present moment require more regular practise over longer time since we have allowed our mind to wander freely for so long.
- Remember that meditation is a very high leverage activity, i.e., more output with less input. There is no other structured activity that can make you more effective in progressing towards your goals. Compare half hour spent on meditation with typical activities like:
  - Reading a newspaper or a technical journal
  - Watching TV
  - Seeing a movie
  - Reading a book

None of them can improve your effectiveness as well as the quality of life as compared to meditation. Meditation helps you to organize your thought process. It helps you to live more effectively in the present moment.
- You may read books, listen to tapes, and listen to discourses on meditation to understand it. The best method of learning meditation is to learn from a master. All the doubts about meditation are answered by practicing it regularly after proper learning.
- Meditation requires patience. We have more than 60,000 thoughts every day and most of them relate to past and future anxieties, leading to stress. Focus in life can be improved significantly through meditation.

Benefits of meditation have been compiled as follows, under the category of physiological, psychological and spirituality by www.ineedmotivation.com/blog/2008/05/100-benefits-of-meditation

Physiological benefits:

1. It lowers oxygen consumption.
2. It decreases respiratory rate.
3. It increases blood flow and slows the heart rate.
4. Increases exercise tolerance.
5. Leads to a deeper level of physical relaxation.
6. Good for people with high blood pressure.
7. Reduces anxiety attacks by lowering the levels of blood lactate.
8. Decreases muscle tension.
9. Helps in chronic diseases like allergies, arthritis, etc.
10. Reduces Pre-menstrual Syndrome symptoms.
11. Helps in post-operative healing.
12. Enhances the immune system.
13. Reduces activity of viruses, and emotional distress.
14. Enhances energy, strength and vigour.
15. Helps with weight loss.
16. Reduction of free radicals, less tissue damage.

17. Higher skin resistance.
18. Drop in cholesterol levels, lowers risk of cardiovascular disease.
19. Improves flow of air to the lungs resulting in easier breathing.
20. Decreases the aging process.
21. Higher levels of DHEAS (Dehydroepiandrosterone).
22. Prevented, slowed or controlled pain of chronic diseases.
23. Makes you sweat less.
24. Cures headaches & migraines.
25. Greater orderliness of brain functioning.
26. Reduces need for medical care.
27. Less energy wasted.
28. More inclined to sports, activities.
29. Significant relief from asthma.
30. Improves performance in athletic events.
31. Normalizes to your ideal weight.
32. Harmonizes your endocrine system.
33. Relaxes your nervous system.
34. Produces lasting beneficial changes in brain electrical activity.
35. Helps cure infertility (the stresses of infertility can interfere with the release of hormones that regulate ovulation).

Psychological benefits:

36. Builds self-confidence.
37. Increases serotonin level, influences mood and behaviour.
38. Resolves phobias and fears.
39. Helps control own thoughts.
40. Helps with focus and concentration.
41. Increases creativity.
42. Increases brain wave coherence.
43. Improves learning ability and memory.
44. Increases feelings of vitality and rejuvenation.

45. Increased emotional stability.
46. Improves relationships.
47. Mind ages at slower rate
48. Easier to remove bad habits.
49. Develops intuition.
50. Increases productivity.
51. Improves relations at home and at work
52. Able to see the larger picture in a given situation.
53. Helps ignore petty issues.
54. Increases ability to solve complex problems.
55. Purifies your character.
56. Develops will power.
57. Greater communication between the two brain hemispheres.
58. Respond more quickly and more effectively to a stressful event.
59. Increases ones perceptual ability and motor performance.
60. Higher intelligence growth rate.
61. Increases job satisfaction.
62. Increases the capacity for intimate contact with loved ones.
63. Decreases potential mental illness.
64. Better, more sociable behaviour.
65. Less aggressiveness.
66. Helps in quitting smoking, alcohol addiction.
67. Reduces need and dependency on drugs, pills, and pharmaceuticals.
68. Need less sleep to recover from sleep deprivation.
69. Require less time to fall asleep, helps cure insomnia.
70. Increases sense of responsibility.
71. Reduces road rage.
72. Decrease in restless thinking.
73. Decreases tendency to worry.
74. Increases listening skills and empathy.

75. Helps make more accurate judgments.
76. Greater tolerance.
77. Gives composure to act in considered and constructive ways.
78. Grows a stable, more balanced personality.
79. Develops emotional maturity.

Spiritual benefits:

80. Helps keep things in perspective.
81. Provides peace of mind, happiness.

http://liveanddare.com/mission/

Summary

- Memory: Self-discipline of the mind to remember to come back to the present.
- Keen interest and passion: To promotes focus on the job at hand now.
- Challenge: To help you to be in state of flow, completely engrossed in the present and leading to personal growth. If the task is too challenging and beyond your skill, then you go into anxiety and frustration. But if it is not challenging enough, you fall into boredom. Stretch yourself, but don't snap. We're at our most effective when in the zone of Flow.
- Concentration: Concentrate on one activity at a time and avoid multi-tasking.
- Control over desires: This leads to higher level of happiness, the ultimate objective of life, dissolving the blocks like anger, grief, fear, greed, pride and attachment
- Clarity of goals and prioritization of activities which are important but not urgent.
- Perseverance towards focused goal.
- Satsang, i.e., company of value based persons, and reading inspiring literature.
- Delegation: For pursuing higher leadership goals and also developing your team for effective implementation of the ideas.

CHAPTER-6

What Else Can Make People Effective?

*I*t is well acknowledged that meditation is the structured technique for developing the quality of mind to be more effective. Actual experience in life shows that many people have demonstrated very high degree of effectiveness, but without any formal learning, training, or practise of meditation. Therefore, there is a logical conclusion that there may be other conditions which may produce results similar to meditation. Let us look at the vast literature on self-effectiveness and understand some of it.

Some of the factors that make people effective are:
1. Memory
2. Keen interest and passion
3. Challenge
4. Concentration
5. Control over desires
6. Dissolving the blocks like anger, grief, fear, greed, pride, and attachment
7. Perseverance towards focused goal
8. *Satsang*, i.e., company of value based persons, reading value based inspiring literature
9. Delegation

1. Memory

It is the nature of the mind to wander. A normal human being entertains more than 60,000 thoughts in a day on a variety of subjects, spread over time and space. In case a person is highly disciplined and he remembers the instructions, come back to the present moment, all the time, then the moment the mind goes away from the task in the present moment, the master command reminds it to come back. If we learn to keep the mind focused on the job at hand by our mental discipline, then we are living in the present moment most of the time and this is precisely one of the objectives of meditation. Therefore, the person with the inbuilt discipline to remind himself to remain in the present moment is already reaping the benefits of meditation. This type of mental discipline is difficult to teach to persons. Take the example of Arjun in *Mahabharata*. He could focus his mind on the target without any diversion.

Memory in this context does not refer to storage of information like 5 GB on a memory stick. It refers to **the inbuilt discipline of the mind to remind itself to come back to the present moment** where the action is.

2. Keen interest and passion

Personal life is neglected often by professionals building their careers. There is a need to examine as to what a person would like to do if he had no need to earn money through a profession. These activities would reveal the deeper values of life and pursuing them would give you happiness in life. Hobbies play a very important role and, incidentally, most of the highly effective persons pursue their hobby in addition to their professional work.

Many people take time off from their work to engage in an activity which they really like and which makes them happy. Such activities may include hobbies that people enjoy. If the hobby is trekking in a jungle, then trekking is not considered a work but a source of joy. Such people may consider "work" as a necessity to earn their living for supporting a family and discharging their obligations in the society. While pursuing their hobby or interest, they are fully engaged in the activity and their mind does not require any external incentive or threat to keep them fully focused on the activity. In life, interests may come and then fade away over a period of time, but a sustained interest may become a passion for a person. Let us take some of the cases when people are engaged in an activity with keen interest.

Watch carefully the young boys and girls in your neighbourhood who are learning how to ride a cycle. Their interest in cycling is very high and at that moment nothing else seems to matter. The children will not feel thirsty or hungry. They will not care about the sun or the wind. Their mind is fully focused on the activity and their mind does not wander to the past events or to the anxiety of the future. This keen interest may be lost when the children have learnt cycling and then they may develop interest in something else, like a newly acquired computer at home. The interests and hobbies keep on changing as you grow. I remember the keen interest of my children in stamp collecting, coin collecting, music (guitar), jungle trekking, bird watching, painting, motor cycling, etc., at different points of time, but none of the activities had a sustained interest for them.

In contrast to above, take the case of Salim Ali. He is regarded as an expert in the area of ornithology. He wrote many books on the subject. One of his famous books is *The Book of Indian Birds*, published by Bombay Natural History Society, 1996. He had a keen interest in observing birds and it became a passion for him. His interest was so strong that he was fully focused when he was watching the birds. Without any formal training on the subject, be became an authority on birds in India. His observations were far superior compared to people who had done research or had PhD in ornithology. He is acknowledged as a highly effective person in the field on ornithology or bird watching. When a person has a passion in an activity, it becomes a mode of meditation, the mind is fully focused, and nothing else seems to matter anymore.

There are many examples like Salim Ali, where persons had a passion towards a subject and this made them really effective in their area. Sachin Tendulkar is an example of a person with passion towards cricket. The passion towards the game made him a highly effective and respected batsman in the world of cricket.

In the area of sports, music, or social service, you can identify highly effective people and they will invariably be persons with a passion towards an activity or a cause. See some of the examples:

- Pele (Football player)
- Sachin Tendulkar (Cricket player from India)
- Nadia Comaneci (Gymnast of Olympic fame)
- Dhyan Chand (an outstanding hockey player from India)
- Baba Amte (Social Service)
- Sunderlal Bahuguna (Environmentalist)
- Vishwanathan Anand (World chess champion)
- Vincent Van Gogh (Dutch painter)
- Leonardo da Vinci (Painter, sculptor, architect, and an innovator)
- Mahatma Gandhi (Freedom fighter and Father of the Nation)

The above people recognized their passion, pursued it and integrated it into their lives to get satisfaction, success, and effectiveness and left their mark on the society. When you have sustained, keen interest in a subject, then

- You are focused on the activity.
- So-called work becomes a sport and becomes a source of joy and bliss with fulfilment.
- You lose track of time.
- You perform beyond your normal skills and capability.
- You don't feel tired; in fact the work gives you the energy (e.g., Mahatma Gandhi).
- You show enthusiasm and develop confidence.

The end result is the work with joy and bliss, leading to effectiveness.

In today's environment, a majority of the people are not engaged in a work or activity where they have keen or passionate interest. The result is a mediocre performance. The careers are chosen not on account of passion or interest but due to various other factors like:

- Peer or group pressure
- Unfulfilled desires of the parents
- The job opportunities, promotions, high salaries, etc.

Highly effective people are essentially engaged in an activity in which they have passionate interest and this gives them great joy. The passion gives them a purpose and a sense of direction in their life. They develop the energy and will power to pursue their goals even when they are faced with setbacks (e.g., Thomas Edison, Mahatma Gandhi, and Swami Vivekananda). The effectiveness through passion for a cause can make a hero out of an ordinary clerk as seen in the Japanese movie "Ikuru" directed by Kurusawa.

According to Tom Rath, the author of the book *Strength Finder*:

- A vast majority of people (around 70%) do not have the opportunity to focus on what they do best.
- People spend more time and efforts in the area of their weakness to overcome the deficiencies.
- Adding raw talent may be possible with considerable effort and time, but it may not make you more effective.
- Most successful people start with their dominant talent and then add skills, knowledge, and practice. When they do this, the raw talent actually serves as a multiplier.
- Talent x investment = strength

- Talent is a natural way of thinking, feeling or behaving.
- Investment is time spent on practicing, developing your skills, and building your knowledge base.
- Strength is the ability to consistently provide near perfect performance.

• For example, a person has natural talent (on scale of 1 to 5) in two areas as follows:
  - A-Cricket - 5 (dominant talent)
  - B-Chemistry - 2 (weak talent)

If he invests best effort of 5 (on a scale of 1 to 5) on A, then his strength is = 25. If he invests best effort of 5 (on a scale of 1 to 5) on B, then his strength is = 10. If the effort is only 2, then the resultant strength would be 10 in A and 4 in B.

• The important learning is that highly effective persons focus more on their dominant talent rather than their weakness area.

Correlate the above with the concept of *Gunas* in Indian philosophy, where persons are classified according to their inherent tendencies: *satvik*, *rajasik* and *tamasik*.

Satvik persons have a long term vision.

Rajasik persons are aggressive and want to win battles.

Tamasik persons have inertia and have to be pushed to perform.

When persons are engaged in their work according to their Gunas, then they are far more effective.

- A tamasik person, by natural tendency, will perform most effective in roles for tamasik persons. Even very heavy investment of effort will not give result in satvik or rajasik areas for such people.

- A rajasik person will not be very effective in tamasik or satvik areas.
- A satvik person will be most effective in satvik areas.

3. Challenge

Challenge is another factor which makes people effective. Let us examine a game of lawn tennis. When you play against an opponent who does not offer any challenge to you and it is very easy for you to win the game, even if you go on playing against that person for a long time, will it improve your game? The chances are rare of improving your skills while playing against a weak player. Let us change the situation to where your opponent is a better player than you and it is rather difficult to win a game. In such a case your game will improve.

When your opponent gives you a tough challenge, then where is your mind while playing? The mind is totally focussed on the game and the incoming ball. You are mentally living in the present moment. Therefore, a challenging game results in threefold benefit:

i) Your game improves (skill).
ii) You enjoy the game.
iii) Your mind gets the practice to remain in the present moment.

The deep purpose behind all competitive games is not limited to making you an expert player but to improve the quality of your mind and giving you joy. You can clearly observe the high degree of awareness of the mind on the game when there is a challenge in it and it requires effort. This explains the importance given to sports in the best schools and colleges.

When a child is learning cycling for the first time, it is a great challenge and the mind is fully engaged in the activity. It amounts to the continuous flow of mind since the mind is fully engaged in the present moment and there is no room for wandering into the past or the future. In case a person is worried (about past experience of falling down from a bike) or having the anxiety or worry that one would fall down, and then the learning would be slowed down. Your mind has to be focused on the activity to learn it.

Mountaineers improve their skill by scaling tough mountains that provide challenge; they will not enjoy scaling a small hill. When a mountaineer is negotiating a steep slope on the edge of a ridge, he is fully concentrating on every step. This, again, amounts to meditation. The joy of mountaineering comes only in overcoming a tough situation. The most memorable and joyful events in the life of a mountaineer are invariably the tough and challenging situations they faced and not the comfortable flat road.

The role of challenge in self-development has been explained in detail through the concept "Flow" by Mihaly Csikzentmihalyi's in his book *Flow: the Psychology of Happiness*, published by Harper and Row. Mihaly developed the theory of optimal experience based on the concept of Flow. He has defined Flow as:

The state in which people are so involved in an activity that nothing else seems to matter; the experience itself is so enjoyable that people will do it even at great cost, for the sake of doing it.

Mihaly Csikzentmihalyi's research is focused on the Flow states that optimize our performance by finding a balance between challenge and skill. If the task is too challenging and beyond our skills, we go into anxiety and frustration, and if it is not challenging enough, we fall into boredom. Stretch yourself, but don't snap. We're at our most effective when in the zone of Flow.

The following diagram shows the model for personal growth in terms of physical and mental skills. It is a modified version of the concept of Flow developed by Mihaly in his book, with inputs from Mohan Lakhamraju.

What Else Can Make People Effective?

For a given level of skill of a person,

- If the person is engaged in an activity that requires lower level of skill, then he gets bored. Boredom leads to lack of focus and poor quality of work. Even prolonged experience of this type of work, which lacks challenge, will not lead to any improvement in the skill of the person. The mind will also wander.
- If the challenge in the task is made larger, this gives adequate challenge to the performer, and then he feels comfortable. This would lead to better work, but it would not improve the skills of the person.
- If the task is slightly more challenging than the skill level of the person, then he feels a little uncomfortable and tries to focus on the challenging task. If the mind is fully involved in this task, then the skill of the person improves. For example, if a high jump athlete goes on practising jumping over the 5 foot bar all the time, then he will not improve his performance until the bar of difficulty is raised gradually to higher levels which would be challenging him. This is a zone of uncomfort, which would stretch the skills of the person to higher levels and the mind would be fully focused on the task.
- If the level of difficulty or challenge is increased to a level which the person is unable to cope with, then this leads to anxiety and frustration because there is failure in performance all the time. This is the zone of stress and would lead to burnouts.
- When a person is involved in an activity which is close to uncomfortable levels, then the following things happen:
  ‣ The skill of the person increases and he can take bigger challenges.
  ‣ The mind is fully involved and focused on the task, leading to high quality output.

- The mind learns to focus on the task.
- The person is in Flow that is, fully involved physically and mentally in the activity. In such a situation the work becomes a worship which leads to self-development in terms of skills and discipline of the mind.

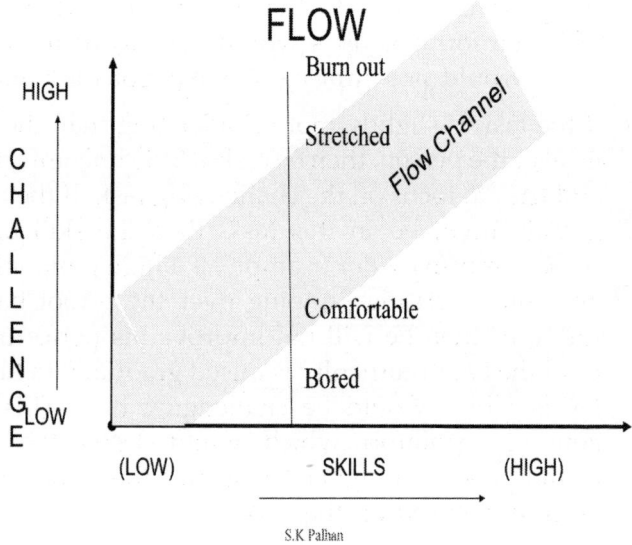

Let us take the case of surgeons at work. You will be surprised to know that surgeons do not enjoy a routine surgery, but when the surgical case is tough and challenging, they forget themselves and their pains or hunger. The challenge of the task focuses their mind on the job and this leads to skill improvement in surgery and the improvement in their focus of mind and joy level.

The Flow activities have the following characteristics:
- The person is fully absorbed mentally in the activity.
- They provide a sense of discovery, a creative feeling of transporting the person into a new reality.

What Else Can Make People Effective?

- They push the person to a higher level of performance.
- They challenge the person adequately, corresponding to the existing skill levels such that it does not lead to boredom or anxiety.
- Flow is a very powerful motivator for an activity.

Flow is similar to the concept of *magna* in Hindi, which means a state of mind in which one is fully involved in an activity, e.g., a Sufi saint singing praise of the Lord, a musician performing a raga in Indian classical music, and pilgrims on a tough trek to Mansarovar and Kailash mountain. All of them are engaged fully (physically and mentally) in the activity, with a sense of joy. They are *magna* in the activity or they are in Flow as described by Mihaly.

I have seen surgery environment from very close quarters. My wife, Santosh, was doing her MD when we were engaged. I spent long hours waiting outside the operation theatre (OT) along with other doctors. My wife developed back pain due to lifting some heavy objects. She recovered through tractions when the pain was acute and later on recovered by doing Yoga and started surgery once again. Prolonged standing started the pain again. I clearly remember that when she was engaged in a challenging surgery like a caesarean section to save a precious child, she was in surgery for 2 to 3 hours at a stretch. She forgot about the pain when she was in the OT and felt it only when the highly focussed task of surgical operation was completed. In fact, this is a typical case of professional who is in Flow at work.

According to Yerkes-Dodson Law developed in 1908, Top performers, highly effective people operate in their focus zone. They called it IZOF, i.e., Individual Zone of Optimal Functioning Attention, which depends on the level of stimulus. Low stimulus is under powered and it leads to low attention. Very high stimulus is overpowered and this also leads to low attention. When the stimulus is just right, then you are in your focus zone and here the attention level is the highest. If you are underpowered, multi-tasking is good and it brings you back to your focus zone. If you are in the overdrive mode, then multi-tasking will make the things worse.

According to Mihaly, extraordinary moments of peak performance are the result of spontaneous effortless Flow. Though seemingly elusive, anyone, not just the athletes and the virtuous, can go into the groove, in the zone, in the Flow, responding instinctively to all the changing elements that used to normally cause him to fail. While in Flow, a person does not think. He acts spontaneously, effortless, smoothly, totally involved in the moment, fully attentive and alert, all his parts and aspects balance and are interacting harmoniously.

Yoga is a thoroughly structured regime for enhancing effectiveness of a person. It generates peak performance in the activity of one's choice, with emphasis on concentration, endurance and performance. Whether training for competition or pleasure, one's enjoyment of the activity is enhanced with regular Yoga practice (asana, prayer, and meditation, all combined together and not in piecemeal). Mental preparation based on yogic techniques imparts the extra edge for competition at the higher level.

4. Focus on one activity at a time (Concentration)

Human mind has infinite potential and it has the capability of multi-tasking also. You can observe people having lunch and also watching TV at the same time, or children studying a book and also simultaneously listening to music. In many places, you may find the driver of a car, with music playing loudly, attending to a call on a mobile phone and also taking some time off to rebuke the motorcyclist overtaking from the wrong side. It is possible to do multiple activities, but the issue is, is it desirable? In the Indian system, the clear-cut direction is that a person should concentrate on one activity at a time. If you are eating, don't talk or watch a movie. For a student who is engaged in reading a book and watching a TV serial at the same time, the mental awareness shifts between the book and the TV alternately. This encourages the flitting of mind from one subject to another and effectiveness is lost in both the activities. If you concentrate on one activity, your mind is focused, whereas in multiple activities you destroy or weaken the power of the mind to concentrate. In fact, it almost amounts to anti-meditation, which would lead to ineffectiveness.

Concentrating on one activity at a time definitely improves the availability of mind for that activity for the first creation. If the mind is fluctuating, then the response to the first creation is also likely to be delayed. This concept can be understood from the analogy of a computer server connected to five nodes. The same server appears to respond to the command of all the five computers simultaneously, but if you analyze it in detail, the server does the task of one computer at a time, but the switching from one computer to another is so fast that all the nodes perceive that the server is attending to them simultaneously, but in the actual case it is an intermittent service. When there are too many demands on the server, then all the systems slow down and the working deteriorates. The same phenomenon happens when the mind is attending to a large number of activities at a time.

There are many compelling cases against multi-tasking. Attention is a finite resource. The inutility of multi-tasking as a productivity tool makes perfect sense when understood in terms of attention and available resources.

"Current cognitive models suggest that people have a limited amount of attention available at any moment," says Seth Greenberg, Professor of Psychology at Union College.

"Attention could be thought of as a fuel that can be dispersed. Thus, tasks can be performed simultaneously with efficiency as long as the required attention for both tasks does not exceed the limit." In other words, a person can multi-task effectively as long as any given task doesn't require too much attention and thereby exhaust his resources.

For example, if worker is engaged in a routine activity which is not challenging, then he can listen to the music or converse with his colleagues at the same time. Similarly, shuttling among two or three different pieces of work can be accomplished efficiently provided each one is relatively simple. In case of creative and challenging tasks it is better to stick to one activity at a time and multi-tasking would lead to inferior performance.

Darrel Raynor, a managing director with Data Analysis & Results, has been aware of multi-tasking's damaging effects on productivity for a number of years.

Raynor, who works with companies to create project management offices as a way of boosting IT productivity, says a database analyst asked to switch among four projects will likely be 45 per cent less productive than if she's allowed to finish one before starting the next.

Multi-tasking has become a way of life now in many organizations. In case the activities are done almost simultaneously, then it affects the performance, since the mind will have the tendency to wander over multiple tasks at hand. Even in the case of multiple tasks at different stages of progress a better alternative is to keep the mind focused on the task which is being performed at any time.

Focusing the mind on one activity at a time leads to discipline of the mind and effectiveness. Parallel operation of activities reduces the focus of mind because the mind is shifting very quickly from one activity to another, which requires additional setting up time to adjust to the new task. Focused sunlight is far more effective than diffused light with same energy level.

5. Control over desires

If a person has a large number of desires, then there are definitely more avenues for the mind to wander. More the desires, more is the fluctuation and wandering of the mind. The modern society is subjected to large number of desires that are inflamed by the vigorous marketing in all the media. In fact, one of the fundamental purposes of marketing is to create strong desire for a product in the target customers so that the customers buy the product to satisfy the desire generated in them. Many marketing experts may find the above statement to be too harsh, but it is the truth. Marketing is really not required to fulfil the needs of the people. It is required only when you want to inflate the desires in people.

When the desires are aggravated by the environment, their satisfaction gives no guarantee of contentment or happiness. Satisfaction of more desires does not reduce, but inflames the desires still further. Suppose, a normal person has 10 desires and he is able to satisfy 7 of them within the time and facilities available to him. If the person is exposed to media, it may increase his desires from 10 to 100. Even if the person is able to satisfy 3 times more number of desires, i.e., 21, the satisfaction level of that person would be only 21% as compared to 70% in the earlier case. Therefore, lesser the number of desires, less is the wandering of the mind and higher is the level of satisfaction. Desires are like mirage and they move forward to a higher level when you pursue them.

Less exposure to desires is highly desirable at a stage when a person is studying to develop the knowledge, skills, and character. The traditional system of learning in ancient India was called the Gurukul. Gurukuls were centred on a knowledgeable and learned person who lived in the forest, without the conveniences or facilities of a city or a palace. The students spent 8 to 10 years in their formative period with the Guru in the forest. The kings could have called the Gurus to teach the princes in the palaces, but this was never done because the dazzle of the palaces would provide more avenues for the distraction of the mind. Everyone understood that the learning environment should be simple, where more desires are not cultivated to distract the mind. The development of the mind, discipline, and values were the main content of the Gurukul education.

It is interesting to note that job skills were given low priority. The son of a king was not taught administration of the kingdom, the son of a warrior was not taught the strategy of wars, the son of a businessman was not taught accounting or the techniques of profit maximization. The students were given the training in discipline, duties, values of life, and development of the mind. The ancient people had realized that if you have a focused mind and sense of duty, you can learn almost any skill for earning your livelihood and living a purposeful life.

We have seen today that the life span of skills has become short. The skills that a software engineer or a medical doctor learned a decade ago are no longer relevant today. If a person has to be effective, he or she must have the capability to learn new skills. This is possible and easier when the mind is well disciplined and has lesser number of desires. The source of happiness is through the performance of duty (Dharma), according to H. H. Jagadguru Bharati Teertha (Shankaracharya of Sringeri Math), a well known authority on Vedanta philosophy. All attempts to get happiness through the satisfaction of inflamed desires are subject to the law of diminishing returns.

The concept of lesser number of desires is not easy to understand when the environment and society is linking more desires with the progress of mankind. The thirst for desires never ends—it inflames the desire further. The final result of having more desires is that the quality of mind reduces and hence the ability to focus and live in the present moment. Highly effective people have better control over their desires. Aristotle from the West and Chanakya from the East have advocated strongly the control over desires for effective leadership. In more recent times, the king of Bhutan has given the concept of "Index of Happiness" and this essentially implies that happiness does not necessarily comes from more goods or services used to satisfy the desires. Higher satisfaction in life comes through the control over desires. (*Gross Happiness Index*, The Centre for Bhutani Studies).

The value system is lost when desires overtake a person. Thus, control over desires is also an important factor, which is conducive for effectiveness.

Control over desires is conducive for effectiveness and satisfaction in life. This reduces the avenues to the mind for wandering, especially in undirected activities.

6. Clarity of goals and prioritization of activities

Highly effective people have very clear goals and their prioritization of activities is focused towards their goals. Working very hard or running very fast may not take you to your goal unless the activities are directed towards the goal. A person may be very active, but the effectiveness comes only when the activities are directed towards the goals.

Many people have hazy goals. The short-term activities, while being attractive, take a person away from the goals. One of the axioms of prioritization is "the long term good against short-term pleasant." Short-term pleasant activities are usually driven by desires and impulses of an undisciplined mind. Perseverance to pursue the goals is a very strong characteristic of highly effective people. E.g., Edison did not give up the efforts to develop an incandescent light bulb in spite of many failures. Mahatma Gandhi did not abandon his goal of freedom for 20 years. He faced many problems and social issues, but he was very clear about his goals. All his activities were directed towards the goal. It was this perseverance that made Mahatma Gandhi the most effective freedom fighter of India.

Stephen Covey has expounded the concept of "long term good against short-term pleasant" further in his book, *The first thing first*. Effective people base their activities from their mission statement of their life. The goals for all the roles a person plays at a particular time need to be clarified first. The roles in life go on changing as a person grows from a child, to a student, professional, employee, and a parent etc. Each role has different goals.

In the Indian philosophy, life has been divided into four stages:
i) Student (*brahmacharya*)
ii) House-holder (*grahastha*)
iii) Delegation (*vaanprastha*)
iv) Renunciation (*sanyas*)

The objectives, duties, and roles at each stage of life have been well defined. Effectiveness of the role will come as a result of the focus on the goals of the respective role. Highly effective people give high priority to activities which are "important and not urgent". Most of their activities are not driven by urgencies because urgencies are decided by external agencies, whereas importance defines the activities, which take us towards our goal.

7. Perseverance

Perseverance is a characteristic of highly effective persons. Take the example of Thomas Edison who did not give up the quest for developing an electric lamp in spite of many failures; ordinary persons would have given up after few failures. We normally see only the success and not the hard work and perseverance in the background. Let us see the following examples:

The Beatles did not become famous just like that. They had sung together at various places for more than 10,000 hours to earn the appreciation of their listeners. Bill Gates is another example of perseverance. When other boys were busy in different activities, he put in more than a thousand hours in writing software programs. The best students in universities did not have so much programing experience at that time. The best students in IITs in India did not have as much experience in programing at that time as compared to Bill Gates. He did not have the facility of a computer in his school and had the drive to get access to the facility at odd hours.

Sachin Tendulkar, India's legendary cricketer, had perseverance to play cricket for a long time, till he was recognized, though at a very young age. Before he played test cricket, he had put in more than ten thousand hours of playing at a very young age.

8. Satsang: The company of good thoughts, people, and books

Good company guides you towards desirable goals in life. The value and priorities get reinforced by it from time to time. Satsang is an important concept in virtually all the religious philosophies of the word — Christianity, Buddhism, Muslims, and Hindu. A man is known by the company he keeps. When a person spends more time in the company of his friends, he acquires their behaviour pattern and value system. Spend more time with learned people; they inspire you to become better person. If you want to be a great sports person, then the company with lazy persons will not make you a star player.

Literally speaking sat means truth and sang means company. The purpose of satang is to develop or acquire better qualities through association with better persons. In Indian ethos persons are classified according to their gunas or natural tendencies i.e. Satvik, Rajasik and Tamasik. Rajasik persons are passionate and driven by restless activity to prove them and achieve victories. Rajasik persons make very good warriors, marketing persons and sportsmen. The tamasik persons are lethargic, they have inertia and an external force is required to push them into action. They are not sensitive to the need of other persons and are usually negative and pessimistic in their approach. They drain away the energy of other persons by raising objections or discouraging them for taking action. They find excuses for not doing an activity. They also have tendency to addictive habits and have extreme mood swings. All persons have some component of the three tendencies and predominance of any quality classifies a person in that category. Satvik persons have long term vision of life, they are more disciplined with lesser desires. They are not self-centred and opt for long term good against short term pleasant activities. They make very good leaders, teachers and research and development professionals. If your company is Satvik then you may acquire satvik qualities in you. People tend to become tamasik in the company of tamasik persons

For personal development it is desirable to spend more time with successful and vale based persons. In institution like IITs, you have the company of brilliant students and you tend to become better. The negative aspects of bad company are more prominent because we tend to pick up bad habits / qualities quicker as compared to good / desirable qualities.

Associate yourself with people of good quality, for it is better to be alone than in bad company.
Peter T. Washington
From good company or Satsang comes non-attachment- that is a certain amount of dispassion for all things worldly. From non-attachment arises freedom from delusion. A person becomes dispassionate when he is free from moha. When there is freedom from delusion, his mind becomes still and from this state he can easily gain liberation. Such is the greatness of satsang.
Adi Shankara in Bhaja Govindam

9. Delegation

Even the best ideas may be of little use until they are implemented. Implementation requires energy and skills in many disciplines. Large ideas require a bigger team for implementation. A team has to be developed to march towards the goals. A person with ideas cannot do everything by himself and that is why most effective people develop their team to achieve the goals. This is where delegation plays an important role. Delegation is primarily about entrusting others. This means that the team members can act and initiate independently and that they assume responsibility with you for certain tasks. An effective person is knowledgeable about the strengths and weaknesses of his team members. Team members are given the opportunity to play a significant role in getting the goal accomplished.

Delegation leads to efficiency and effectiveness. Many people refuse to delegate to others; they feel it takes too much time and effort and they could do the job better themselves. Thus, they have little time for using their full potential for creative work. The purpose of delegation is to use skills and resources already within the group. Highly effective persons use delegation to develop new leaders and build new skills within the group to get things done. They encourage the team to feel a part of the effort and the success and free up their time to focus on other initiatives. This also leads to increased flexibility.

Delegation has to be done very carefully since it will not be effective if it is done as a punishment or for dumping of tasks on the members who are not provided adequate resources, skills, and authority.

Sometimes tasks are given to team members but there is constant detailing out of instructions. This is called *puppeteering* and it is not delegation. Effective delegation involves clear up-front mutual understanding and commitment regarding expectations in the following five areas:

- Desired results which are clear and understood by both sides.
- Guidelines which identify parameters, restrictions, established practices or values, and pitfalls if known.
- Identify the human, financial, technical and organizational resources that can be drawn upon.
- Accountability and standard of performance to be used for evaluation.
- Positive or negative consequences of evaluation.

Effective delegation makes you more effective and relaxed. It gives you opportunity for personal growth towards higher functions in the organization. It helps to grow your team members, which is one of the important responsibilities of a leader. Most of the highly effective persons use delegation to achieve effectiveness. Mr. Shridharan (CMD of Delhi Metro Corporation) believed in effective delegation to develop a highly motivated and effective team for execution, which led to highly successful implementation of Delhi metro.

Summary

There are a large numbers of techniques for meditation. The techniques may be classified under the following categories:
- Ancient meditations
- Techniques popular in India
- Western adaptation of meditation

Brief on some of the techniques of meditations is given at *Appendix 2*

Chapter -7

Types of Meditations

*M*editation is not necessarily a religious practice, but because of its spiritual element it forms an integral part of most religions. And even though the basic objective of most meditation styles remain the same and are performed in a state of inner and outer stillness, they all vary according to the specific religious framework within which they are placed. Preparation, posture, length of period of meditation, particular verbal or visual elements—all contribute to the various forms of meditation. Some of the more popular methods are: Transcendental Meditation, *yoga nidra*, *vipassana*, and mindfulness meditation.

It was not till the 20th century that a need for the creation of secular forms of popular meditation techniques began to be felt. But for the most part, these meditation systems were little more than rehashed versions of older techniques, which had been extracted from their religious contexts. Transcendental Meditation (TM), as propagated by Maharishi Mahesh Yogi, is one such version which grew out of the Hindu practice of *naam japa*.

There are many schools and styles of meditation within Hinduism. Yoga is generally done to prepare one for meditation, and meditation is done to realize union of one's self, one's atman, with the Omnipresent and non-dual Brahman. This experience is referred to as moksha by Hindus and is similar to the concept of nirvana in Buddhism. The earliest clear references to meditation in Hindu literature are in the middle Upanishads and the Mahabharata, which includes the Bhagavad Gita.

Within Patañjali's ashtanga yoga practice, there are eight limbs leading to kaivalya "aloneness". These are ethical discipline (yamas), rules (niyamas), physical postures (āsanas), breath control (prā□āyama), withdrawal from the senses (pratyāhāra), one-pointedness of mind (dhāra□ā), meditation (dhyāna), and finally samādhi, which is often described as the realization of the identity of the Self (ātman) with the Omnipresent (Brahman), and is the ultimate aim of all Hindu yogis.

Meditation in Hinduism is practised in different forms by different schools and sects and has expanded beyond Hinduism to the West.

The influential modern proponent of Hinduism, who first introduced Eastern philosophy to the West in the late 19th century, Swami Vivekananda, describes meditation as follows:

> Meditation has been laid stress upon by all religions. The meditative state of mind is declared by the Yogis to be the highest state in which the mind exists. When the mind is studying the external object, it gets identified with it, loses itself. To use the simile of the old Indian philosopher: the soul of man is like a piece of crystal, but it takes the colour of whatever is near it. Whatever the soul touches . . . it has to take its colour. That is the difficulty. That constitutes the bondage.

There are varieties of meditation techniques which range from ancient Buddhist to Taoist and Hindu practices. Meditation should be learnt under the guidance of a Guru.

It is very difficult to give details of all types of meditations due to limited knowledge. The well known techniques may be grouped under the following headings (the list is not exhaustive):

- *Ancient meditation techniques*
  - Raj yoga
  - Buddhist

- Zen
- Tao
- Japa
- Mantra
- Chakra
- Hong sau
- Preksha dhyan
- Vipassana
- Soham
- Kabbalah

- **Techniques popular in India**
  - Art of living
  - Sahaj Samadhi
  - Yogananda kriya
  - Sikh meditation
  - Sufi meditation
  - Yog nidra

- **Western adaptations of meditation**
  - Transcendental meditation
  - Kriya yoga
  - Mindfulness
  - Heart centred
  - Guided meditation
  - Trataka meditation
  - Coherence meditation
  - Sedona method

Some of the techniques are described briefly in *Appendix 2*.

Summary

- A large number of scientific studies have been done in the western countries and India on the effects of different types of meditation.
- Some of the studies are not valid statistically but most of them have reported positive effects of different types of meditation for different sample sizes.
- Over 350 research studies have been done at more than 250 universities in the west. Most of the studies relate to Transcendental Meditation.
- Research has been done at All India Institute of Medical Sciences (AIIMS) on *Sudarshan kriya* meditation.
- Research by Dr. Manchanda (a cardiologist from AIIMS and Gangaram Hospital, New Delhi) has been done on the effect of *Preksha Dhyan*
- Research on *Vipassana* has been done by IIT Delhi.
- Research by Mind Body Medical Institute has been done on the relaxation response of meditation.

Chapter -8

Scientific Studies on Effectiveness of Different Types of Meditations

Over 350 research studies have been conducted at more than 250 universities and medical schools (including Harvard, UCLA, and Stanford) on the different types of meditations. These studies have been published and peer-reviewed in more than 100 scientific journals. In India also, research has been carried out on the effects of meditation.

Scientific studies on impact of meditation

Scientific studies have conclusively proved the benefits of meditation for our mind and body. According to search results released by the University of Wisconsin-Madison, meditation has been shown to produce lasting beneficial changes in immune-system function as well as brain electrical activity. "Researchers found about 50 per cent more electrical activity in the left frontal regions of the brains of the meditators. Other research has showed that part of the brain is associated with positive emotions and anxiety reduction." Research on the effects of different types of meditation has been published by the following organizations in the West:
- Mehmet Oz, M.D., Emmy Award-winning host of The Dr. Oz Show
- National Institute of Health, USA
- The American Journal of Cardiology

- Journal of Psychiatry
- American Journal of Hypertension
- Journal of Counselling and Development
- Alcoholism Treatment Quarterly
- Journal Of Clinical Psychology
- Cedar-Sinai Medical Centre, Los Angeles, USA.
- UCLA Medical School
- National Institute Of Health In Bethesda, Maryland
- University of California at Irvine
- Mind Body Medical Institute affiliated to Harvard University and Boston hospitals
- Harvard Medical School
- Yale, Harvard, Massachusetts General Hospitals
- Heart Math Institute

In India, research on meditation has been carried out at AIIMS and Gangaram Hospital at New Delhi and at many other institutions in the country. The details of the research done on Preksha Dhyan, Vipassana and Sudarshan Kriya are given below.

1. Study of pulmonary and autonomic functions of asthma patients after yoga training

Khanam A. A., Sachdeva U, Guleria R, Deepak K. K. Department of Physiology, All India Institute of Medical Science, New Delhi.

A study was conducted with nine diagnosed bronchial asthma patients. Yoga training was given for seven days in a camp in Adhyatma Sadhana Kendra, New Delhi. The autonomic function tests to measure the parasympathetic reactivity (Deep Breathing test, Valsalva Manoeuvre), sympathetic reactivity (Hand Grip test, Cold Pressure test), and pulmonary function tests FVC, FEV1, PEFR, PIF, BHT and CE were recorded before and after yoga training.

The results closely indicated the reduction in sympathetic reactivity and improvement in the pulmonary ventilation by way of relaxation of voluntary inspiratory and expiratory muscles. The "comprehensive yogic life style change programme for patients of Bronchial Asthma" have shown significant benefit even within a short period.

Indian J Physiology Pharmacology, 1996 Oct; 40 (4):318-24

2. Research by Dr. S. C. Manchanda

Dr. Manchanda, a cardiologist, researched many Yoga practices and eventually found that Preksha Meditation was the easiest and best method. He also researched on Preksha Meditation for reversal of heart diseases. He found that Preksha Meditation is extremely powerful to the extent that patients with three blocked arteries could manifest reversal and avoid by-pass surgery. More than 80,000 patients have been saved from heart surgeries through Preksha Meditation techniques.

Dr. Manchanda has also conducted first international study (1997) from AIIMS to substantiate the effects Preksha Dhyan with angiographic proof. For the research, people were selected in the age group of 30–75 years, with chronic stable angina and those who had more than 70 per cent of heart blockage as shown in angiography.

The patients were subjected to Preksha Meditation and also a good diet, moderate aerobic physical exercise and yoga. After few months their vitals were compared to those who were not doing Preksha Meditation. The results were very astonishing. "The progression of cause of blockage in artery stopped and their regression achieved by 15 per cent. Similarly, lipid profile of research group showed 20 per cent improvement. Moreover, procedure in the active group was reduced by approximately 90 per cent. At the end of the study, it was revealed that lifestyle interventions, especially yoga, retarded further complications, improved quality of life and proved to be a cost effective practical method with high degree of compliance."

3. Effect of Vipassana Meditation on quality of life, subjective well-being and criminal propensity among inmates of Tihar jail, Delhi

Final report submitted to Vipassana Research Institute by Dr. Amulya Khurana and Prof. P. L. Dhar, Indian Institute of Technology, New Delhi, June 2000.

This study aimed at investigating the effects of Vipassana Meditation (VM) on Quality of Life (QOL), Subjective Well-Being (SWB), and Criminal Propensity (CP) among inmates of Tihar Jail, Delhi. To this effect the following hypotheses were formulated:
1. There will be a significant positive effect of VM on the QOL of inmates of Tihar jail.
2. VM will have a positive and significant effect on SWB of inmates.
3. Criminal propensity (CP) of inmates will decrease significantly after attending the VM course.
4. There will be significant difference in SWB and CP of experimental (Vipassana) group and control (non-Vipassana) group.
5. Male and female inmates will differ significantly in SWB and CP, as a result of VM.

The total sample comprised 262 inmates (males = 232, females = 30). A series of 5 studies were conducted using both before-and-after as well as control group experimental designs.

The independent variable was Vipassana meditation. The dependent variables were: Quality of life (QOL), Subjective Well-Being (SWB), and Criminal Propensity (CP). Life Satisfaction Scale (PGI, Chandigarh), Subjective Well-Being Scale (Nagpal & Sell, 1985), and Criminal Propensity Scale (Sanyal & Kathpalia, 1999) were used to collect data. Student's "t" test was used for data analysis.

The following conclusions represent the findings of the study:

1. The first hypothesis did not come as was expected. Since the questionnaire was difficult for the prisoners to understand, this questionnaire was dropped from the later studies.
2. The second and third hypothesis were accepted since the level of criminal propensity came down and that of subjective well-being went up after the inmates attended the Vipassana meditation courses.
3. The fourth hypothesis was also accepted, as the experimental (Vipassana) group's CP decreased and SWB increased significantly as compared to control (non-Vipassana) group, among male inmates.
4. VM seems to have similar effect on SWB and CP of participants irrespective of their gender. Thus, the fifth hypothesis was not accepted as the male and female inmates did not differ significantly in SWB and CP, as a result of VM.

The results obtained supported the hypotheses to a large extent, though not all the results are significant. Vipassana meditation significantly improved Subjective well-being and reduced Criminal propensity of inmates of Tihar Jail.

4. Research by Dr. M. Bhatia, Assoc. Prof. Clinical Neurophysiology, Department of Neurology, All India Institute of Medical Sciences, New Delhi

Introduction

Sudarshan Kriya (SK) (a rhythmic breathing process), was devised by Sri Sri Ravi Shankar. The word "Sudarshan" translated from its original Sanskrit Su = right, Darshan = Vision; "Kriya" means purifying action. This is, thus, not a pure meditation technique, and has been defined as a state of relaxation by some and a state of consciousness by others. This is practised as a brief and practical self-help stress management strategy. Subjective reports from the participants indicate that it reduces anxiety and depression and SK has been found to be useful in the treatment of depression. Various tools have been used to study the effect of relaxing techniques on the mind. These include EEG, evoked potentials (BAER, P300, Middle latency potentials), EMRI, SPECT. EEG has been used to study changes during meditation, and also long-term effect of regular practice of meditation for the past 2-3 decades.

The aim of the present study was to study the sequential changes in EEG, during the SK.

Study Design and Methodology

Five regular practitioners of SK formed the study group. They were connected with Ved Vignan Maha Vidya Peeth, who regularly practiced and taught SK. They had attended the basic course (22 hours), advanced course (4 days) and the teachers training course. All were females, with age range from 35 to 45 years, with similar socioeconomic background and education. None had a psychiatric illness, neurologic illness, and none of the subjects were on chronic medications. All the subjects were asked not to take any central nervous system stimulants/ caffeine prior to the test.

Results

Coherence: An increase in coherence was observed in the 6th Cycle, predominantly in the fronto-central regions in the beta band, and posteriorly in the alpha band.
Frequency Analysis: There was an increased alpha activity posteriorly during the SK. In addition a central midline theta activity was observed. The resting EEG demonstrated an increased focal beta activity. GSR Increase was observed during the SK.

Discussion

The increased coherence suggests increased connectivity. This is suggestive of more efficient information processing. The central midline theta activity, and increase in GSR suggests activation and the increased alpha is suggestive of relaxation.

Thus there is a combination of relaxation and activation during the SK.
A larger number of subjects need to be studied to define these changes further.

Scientific evidence that Transcendental Meditation works

"TM dramatically reduces high blood pressure. It also reduces cholesterol, atherosclerosis, obesity, risk of stroke — even lowers death rates due to cardiovascular disease. But this is just the tip of the iceberg. There are so many other benefits to mind and body."

www.umassmed.edu/content.aspx/id=41252

Mehmet Oz, M.D., Emmy Award-winning host of The Dr. Oz Show:

Hundreds of scientific studies have been conducted on the benefits of the Transcendental Meditation program at more than 200 independent universities and research institutions worldwide over the past 40 years. The National Institutes of Health USA have awarded over $26 million to research the effectiveness of TM for reducing stress and stress-related illness, with a focus on cardiovascular disease. Findings have been published in leading, peer-reviewed scientific journals, including *The American Journal of Cardiology* and the American Heart Association's *Hypertension* and *Stroke*.
Research summary shows the following benefits to different category of persons:
- Benefits to Education
  - 21% increase in high school graduation rate
  - 10% improvement in test scores and GPA
  - Increased attendance and decreased suspensions for high school students
  - Reduced ADHD symptoms and symptoms of other learning disorders (*Mind & Brain: The Journal of Psychiatry*)

- Increased intelligence and creativity *(Intelligence* 29: 419-440, 2001)
- 40% reduction in psychological distress, including stress, anxiety and depression *(American Journal of Hypertension* 22(12): 1326–1331, 2009)

• Benefits to Veterans
- 40–55% reduction in symptoms of PTSD and depression *(Military Medicine* 176 (6): 626-630, 2011)
- 42% decrease in insomnia *Journal of Counseling and Development* 64: 212-215, 1985
- 25% reduction in plasma cortisol levels *(Hormones and Behavior* 10: 54–60, 1978)
- Decreased high blood pressure—on par with first-line antihypertensive *(American Journal of Hypertension* 21: 310–316, 2008)
- 47% reduced risk of cardiovascular-related mortality *(Circulation: Cardiovascular Quality and Outcomes* 5: 750-758, 2012)
- 30% improvement in satisfaction with quality of life *(Military Medicine* 176 (6): 626-630, 2011)

• Benefits to Abused Women and Girls
- Reduced flashbacks and bad memories *(Military Medicine* 176 (6): 626-630, 2011)
- Greater resistance to stress *(Psychosomatic Medicine* 35: 341–349, 1973)
- Twice the effectiveness of conventional approaches for reducing alcoholism and substance abuse *(Alcoholism Treatment Quarterly* 11: 13-87, 1994)
- 42% decrease in insomnia *(Journal of Counseling and Development* 64: 212-215, 1985)
- Twice as effective as other relaxation techniques for decreasing trait anxiety *(Journal of Clinical Psychology* 45(6): 957–974, 1989)

- Improved quality of life *(Military Medicine* 176 (6): 626-630, 2011)

Research at Universities and Medical Schools

Research has been conducted on Transcendental Meditation program at 250 independent universities and medical schools, their findings are summarized below:

i. University of Connecticut, USA

At-risk adolescents reduce stress, anxiety and hyperactivity through Transcendental Meditation.
Robert Colbert, PhD, Assistant Professor of Educational Psychology, University of Connecticut, *Annual Meeting of the Society for Behavioral Medicine*, March 2008.

ii. American University, Washington DC

Transcendental Meditation produces positive effects on health, brain functioning and cognitive development in students.
This two-year study of 250 students attending American University and surrounding colleges in Washington, D.C., found that the TM program produced beneficial effects for health, brain functioning and cognitive development compared to the control group.

David Haaga, PhD, Professor and Director of the James J. Gray Psychotherapy Training Clinic, American University, *American Journal of Hypertension*, 2009; *International Journal of Psychophysiology*, 2009

iii. Cedars-Sinai Medical Center, Los Angeles, USA

Transcendental Meditation reduces hypertension, obesity and diabetes in patients with coronary heart disease.
This study of 103 people with coronary heart disease found that individuals practicing Transcendental Meditation for four months had significantly lower blood pressure, improved blood glucose and insulin levels (which signify reduced insulin resistance), and more stable functioning of the autonomic nervous system compared to controls.

C. Noel Bairey Merz, MD, Director of the Preventive and Rehabilitative Cardiac Center at Cedars-Sinai Medical Center; Professor of Medicine at the UCLA Medical School, American Medical Association's *Archives of Internal Medicine*, June 2006

iv. Medical College of Georgia, USA

Reduced high blood pressure among high school students. This eight-month study of 156 hypertensive African American high school students found that the Transcendental Meditation programme reduced high blood pressure among the meditating students as compared with little or no change in the control group (20 per cent of African American teenagers suffer from high blood pressure).

Vernon Barnes, PhD, physiologist and research scientist, Georgia Prevention Institute, Medical College of Georgia, *American Journal of Hypertension*, April 2004

v. University of Michigan, USA

Transcendental Meditation reduces stress and increases happiness among middle school students.
Rita Benn, PhD, Director of Education, Complementary & Alternative Medicine Research Center, University of Michigan. National Institutes of Health in Bethesda, Maryland, April 2003

vi. University of California at Irvine, USA

Transcendental Meditation reduces the brain's reaction to stress. David Orme-Johnson, PhD, study director, Neuroimaging Laboratory, University of California at Irvine, *Neuro Report*, August 2006.

The relaxation response of meditation has been confirmed by the following studies:
1. Dr Herbert Benson, founder of the Mind-Body Medical Institute, which is affiliated to Harvard University and several Boston hospitals, reports that meditation induces

a host of biochemical and physical changes in the body collectively referred to as the "relaxation response".

2. According to a March 2006 article in *Psychological Bulletin*, EEG activity begins to slow as a result of the practice of meditation. The human nervous system is composed of a parasympathetic system, which works to regulate heart rate, breathing and other involuntary motor functions, and a sympathetic system, which arouses the body, preparing it for vigorous activity.

3. Meditation has entered the mainstream of healthcare as a method of stress and pain reduction. As a method of stress reduction, meditation has been used in hospitals in cases of chronic or terminal illness to reduce complications associated with increased stress that include depressed immune. There is growing agreement in the medical community that mental factors such as stress significantly contribute to a lack of physical health, and there is a growing movement in mainstream science to fund research in this area.

4. A 2003 meta-analysis found that MBSR (Mindfulness Based Stress Reduction) was to be helpful in **chronic** pain, fibromyalgia, cancer patients and coronary artery disease. Improvements were noted in both physical and mental health.

5. Mindfulness meditation, anapanasati, and related techniques, are intended to train attention for the sake of provoking insight. A wider, more flexible attention span makes it easier to be aware of a situation, easier to be objective in emotionally or morally difficult situations, and easier to achieve a state of responsive, creative awareness or "flow".

6. A study done by Yale, Harvard and Massachusetts General Hospitals have shown that meditation increases grey matter in specific regions of the brain and may slow the deterioration of the brain as a part of the natural aging process.

Summary

Self-effectiveness is promoted through the combination of the following:
- Regular practise of the meditation which suits the person
- Memory and self- discipline of the mind
- Keen interest and passion
- Challenge to remain in flow
- Concentration on one activity at a time even during multi-tasking
- Proper control over desire and dissolving blocks like anger, grief, fear, greed, pride and attachment
- Perseverance for march towards the goal
- Company of value based people with positive energy
- Delegation for leveraging an effective team for achieving the lofty goals

Chapter-9

Conclusion

Self-effectiveness has been a subject of discussion from ancient times. Different civilizations gave stress to different things to make humans more effective. This led to setting up of educational and training institutions all over the world. Europeans had their guild system to develop persons in different professions. Ancient Indian society had the system *guru shishya prampara* where managing self was given a higher priority over the job skills. In modern times, the stress of the education system is mostly on developing job and professional skills. The mind has not been a subject of discussion in the modern education systems of schools and universities.

The seed for any activity has its beginning in the thought process, which takes place in the mind. It has been proven without doubt that skills alone cannot develop more effective persons. Skills are, no doubt, required for performing any activity, but most of effectiveness is not on account of skills alone; mind plays a very important role in all creative work. The mind has the tendency to wander to the past as well as future and also to undirected activities which reduce its effectiveness. It is known to all that if your mind is fully focused on a task, then the task is performed better. For highly effective and creative work, the mind should be fully focused on the task at hand. To keep the mind in the present moment, the conventional education system does not have any effective tool. Meditation helps persons to focus their minds and make them more effective.

All human beings have infinite potential but the right combination of skill, focus of mind and values leads to self-effectiveness. The role of meditation is to achieve the ultimate objective of life, which is happiness. Self-effectiveness is a by-product and not the ultimate goal of meditation.

A large amount of scientific research done in various parts of the world has shown that meditation techniques lead to more effective performance in different areas. This is one of the reasons for the popularity of meditation all over the world. The interest in meditation can be gauged from the fact that a Google search for meditation would give you more than 128 million references to meditation. It has been estimated that more than 10 million persons practise some type of meditation.

Meditation is one of the best structured techniques to keep the mind in the present moment, where the action is taking place.

Many people have become highly effective in their life without doing any meditation. They have adopted other factors which lead to their deep engagement in the chosen activity. Personal discipline of the mind is very important. The mind has the tendency to wander to the past, future or undirected activities. Therefore, mental discipline to come back soon to the present moment is an important factor. Keen interest or passion in the subject helps them to so in the activity and this factor is common among all highly effective persons. Another issue is the challenge in the task, which makes them focused on the activity without boredom or excess anxiety. Highly effective persons may have multiple interests but they have the capability to focus on the activity at hand. Multi-tasking is not the ideal solution for improving self-effectiveness but when it is unavoidable, even then it is highly desirable to keep the mind focused on the activity being performed at that time There are exceptions like Leonardo Da Vinci, who has shown effectiveness in diversified disciplines like science, mathematics, humanities and arts. Control over desires also helps towards effectiveness. Perseverance is

Conclusion

another common feature in almost all highly effective persons and this is promoted by self-discipline, keen interest and control over desires.

Most of the factors discussed so far are for personal effectiveness, but when the goal requires a lot of energy and manpower resources, managerial techniques like delegation also help to achieve a multiplier effect through proper delegation in the team.

Meditation and other techniques, when applied together, lead to far more self-effective life by achieving lofty goals for the society and the ultimate goal of happiness for self.

Appendix 1

Vedantic Understanding of Mind

Understanding of Mind (*Antaha-karan*) in Vedanta

(Based on lectures by Swami Parmananda Bharati and inputs from Mr. Sunil Kumar)
Within the gross body is the subtle body, consisting of *praana*, Sense organs, and an Inner-instrument, *Antaha-karan* or Mind. The constituents are:
- Five organs of knowledge;
- Five organs of action;
- Five forms in which *praana* which manifests in the body; and
- Inner-instrument or Mind, consisting of:
    - Manas: The function of mind, which inputs the data from sense-organs
    - Chitta: The function of mind where all the past impressions are stored
    - Buddhi: The function of mind which decides and determines
    - Ahamkaara: The function of mind which creates the idea of 'I'-sense

The subtle body is also material and so it cannot also act independently and needs consciousness — *chetana* — to push it into actions.

Appendix 1

Antaha-karan, Inner instrument:

i) The instrument to help the *jiva* experience or perform anything is called *karana*. We will briefly discuss how perception takes place.

The eyes, ears, etc., are the five external instruments of perception or sense-organs, through which the inputs come from outside. These inputs are received by the corresponding organ of each of the five external instruments; even then perception does not take place. The mind as, Manas, must be available to cognize the inputs and Buddhi should be there to decide on what these inputs are, which it does based on past memories, stored in the mind, Chitta.

But, who actually perceives all these inputs coming at lightning speeds? And this entity must be a changeless, conscious entity, to cognize the ever changing pulsations we get every moment. This entity is the atman, the soul, the Self.

It is the eyes, ears, etc., the external instruments, which first absorb the *vishaya*, things of *jagat*. Before these are presented to the *jiva* for its 'experience, enjoyment', *bhoga*, there is an instrument, which does its *vishlesan* or analysis. That inner instrument, which does this *vishlesan*, is antaha-karan, mind. This antaha-karan is made up of all the five *tan-maatraa*, so that it can analyze all five elements, in the incoming vishaya, input-data, and this mind has to be present for cognition to take place.

Shruti explains it thus: "The mind was elsewhere, so I did not see; the mind was elsewhere, so I did not hear"; it is through the mind that we see, it is through the mind we hear. Since we cannot know many things at the same time, it shows that the mind is needed. We may be reading, with our eyes on the book, but may not see some lines; we may be hearing a lecture, but may not listen. The reason is that our Manas was busy elsewhere at that time. Instead of focusing on the *vishaya* it was thinking of something else.

ii) The *antaha-karan* has four functions:
- That which deliberates is the Manas, *Sankalpa-vikalpa*.
- That which makes decisions is Buddhi, *nishchayaatmika buddhi*.
- That where all past memories are stored, is Chitta, *dharanaatmakam chittam*.
- That buddhi, which causes identification of the jiva with the body, mind, karma, etc., is *Ahamkaara, ahamkaroteeti ahamkar*.

They have their respective places in the body: throat, mouth, navel and heart. This *bhaavanaa*, feeling, arising out of misidentification or identification with the body, sometimes gives rise to *durahamkar*, egoistic feelings of "I am rich, I am intelligent".

Sankalpa or resolve precedes each action. *Sankalpa, nishchaya*, decision to act on it, and the consequent memory: I have done this action — I am the doer, knower, enjoyer — this feeling creates an invisible impression on the mind-stuff or antah-karan. A seeker, if by his sincere strivings, attains *gyana* and *moksha*, then this *karma-phala* or fruit of his action, will also be similarly stored up in his antah-karan.

iii) It is our food that we intake, which provides energy to the mind. The gross part of food comes out as waste; the middle becomes flesh and the extremely subtle part forms and nurtures the mind, and so, it is material, *jada*.

If we do not eat *anna*, food, regularly, our power of decisions, power of memory, etc. are weakened. Not only this, the actions of mind depend on the quality of food. Depending on whether our food is *satvik, rajasik or tamasik*, the mind similarly acquires these qualities.

And, therefore it is very important for spiritual-seekers, *sadhak*, to follow regular rules and discipline to ensure that their food, aahaar remains satvik. It is very important to note that *aahaar* is not just food; it also includes all the karma and its phala or information that we absorb through our sense organs. It is therefore essential that we intake only that karma, which does not produce *raga-dwesh* and *moha*. It then leads to vairagya, a quality necessary for *gyaana*, in due course.

Emergence of the Mind in Creation

All material objects, i.e., the *jagat*, is made up of 8 *tattvas* or elements. These are:
- The 5 *Tanmatras* (the elemental-building-blocks of the entire universe according to the Vedas):
    - *Prithvi* (earth)
    - *Aapa* (water)
    - *Agni* (fire/sight)
    - *Vayu* (air)
    - *Akasha* (space)
- *Samasht-mana*, the universal Mind
- *Samasht-buddhi*, the universal Intellect
- *Samasht-ahamkara*, the universal "I" or ego-sense

Ishwara creates *jagat* through his *maya* with the 5 *tanmatras*, building-blocks, associating himself with the universal Mind, which contains the record of the karmas done by the jivas in the previous cycle of creation. The jivas do karma because of their avidya. Since Ishwara has created jagat for the sake of giving opportunity to the jivas to experience the consequent karma-phalas of the karma done by them, this Maya, coupled with Avidya, is treated as the ahamkara, ego-sense of Ishwara.

Process of Sristhi, Projection or Creation and Pralaya

We will now see how projection of jagat takes place. As we have seen, this jagat is built with the 5 Tanmatras. Tanmatras

mean "only that". Each element has only one guna or quality, as follows:
- Prithvi (earth): *Gandha-guna* or smell only
- Aapa (water): *Rasa-guna* or taste only
- Agni (fire/sight): *Roopa-guna* or form only
- Vayu (air): *Sparsha-guna* or touch only
- Akash (space): *Shabda-guna* or sound only

The 5 tanmatras along with Samasthi-mana, the universal mind, Samasthi-buddhi, and *Samasthi-ahamkara*, the universal "I" or ego-sense, are first to manifest. These are the seed of future jagat. Samasthi-buddhi is also called *mahat-tatva*. That Brahman, which is revealed by this upadhi, is called *Hiranya-garbha*, who associates himself with the Samasthi-buddhi. It is this seed of jagat, which evolves as the first body, and is called Praja-pati Brahman or Virat-purusha. It is he who has the responsibility to manage the further process of *sristhi-stithi-laya* or projection of jagat. His one-day includes *sristhi-stithi* and one-night is laya.

It is this Praja-pati Brahman who is responsible for the projection of this inert jagat and also giving birth to all the living beings, based on their karmas, from the highest devataas to the lowest insects, bacteria, etc.

Inside each living being there is a subtle-body. Each living being has 5 pranaas or life-force, all of which have vayu tanmatra. It has 5 Gyanendriyas or organs of knowledge, each having one tanmatra:
- Nose has only Prithvi (earth) as tanmatra: Gandha-guna or smell
- Tongue has only Aapa (water) as tanmatra: Rasa-guna or taste
- Eye has only Agni (fire/sight) as Tanmatra: Roopa-guna or form
- Skin has only Vayu (air) as tanmatra: Sparsha-guna or touch

Appendix 1

- Ear has only Akash (space) as tanmatra: Shabda-guna or sound

Each living being also has 5 karmeyndriyas or organs of action:
- Speech, Vaak, has only agni tanmatra
- Hand, Pani, has only vayu tanmatra
- Feet, Paada, has only akash tanmatra
- Paayu has only prithvi tanmatra
- Upastha has only aapa tanmatra

The mind consists of a combination of all the 5 tanmatras and is, therefore, the coordinator of all these. This process of projection of jagat is called "Panchi-karana". The 5 tanmatras combine together to create 5 Bhootas we experience, which are the gross forms of the 5 tanmatras. The sequence is as follows:
- Akash is created first. It has shabda-guna. It is also the space in which the jagat is accommodated.
- This akaasha combines with vayu tanmatra and its own sparsha guna combines with shabda guna of akaasha and becomes the panchi-krit vayu.
- This vayu combines with agni tanmatra and its own roopa-guna combines with the previous 2 gunas and becomes panchi-krit agni.
- This agni merges with jala tanmatra and its own rasa-guna mixes with previous 3 gunas and becomes panchi-krit jala.
- This jala merges into prithvi tanmatra and its own gandha-guna mixes with previous 4 gunas and becomes prithvi.

Even after this process, the Bhootas do not leave their swaroopa of Brahman. For example, explaining the creation process from the stage of jala or water, Brahman thinks let me take many forms and let me become manifest. From prithvi emerge trees and plants, from which comes food and from food comes semen, *veerya*, which gives birth to humans and living beings with gross bodies. From the creator Brahma to every being, each and every being takes birth based on their respective karmas which they have themselves performed in the previous kalpa.

To initiate this process of Panchikaran and create these various names and forms, the prompting or pravritti, is in the samasthi ahamkara of Hiranyagarbha. He is Ishwara. The prompting or pravritti in him to project the jivas and jagat comes from the Avidya of the jivas. This remains hidden in the unmanifested, avyakta.

Since pravritti or prompting is the sign or lakshana of ahamkara, this avyakta, enjoined with the Avidya, is itself ahamkara. Just as food mixed with poison is itself called poison, so, the ahamkara, which is like poison because of Avidya, when it mixes with avyakta, is called ahamkara. Thus, even though the prompting has come because of the Avidya of the jivas, the ability is of avyakta itself, which is Parameshwara himself. This prakriti is lower because it is mixed with Avidya.

In this way, this projected Jagat remains till the end of this cycle; at its end is *pralaya*, when it dissolves. The sequence of destruction is the exact opposite of its projection. Panchikrit bhootas merge back into the very bhootas from which they had emerged. The Jivas merge into earth, the earth into jala, the jala into agni, the agni into vayu, the vayu into akaasha, and the akaasha merges back into Parabrahman.

We Are Equal as Spirit but Unequal as Body-Minds

Identified with the body-mind complex, we are all different. We are equal only when we learn and practise identifying ourselves with the Spirit, Atman, within us. My mind-set, my worldview, is being continuously formed, deformed or refined, every moment by my thought-actions, my karmas, e.g., my Governing Values, beliefs, motives, thoughts, goals, choices, words and actions. Results of our Karma remain in our mind as impressions, *samskaras*, in the form of a) tendency or desire to repeat an action and b) the memory of the Karma.

Every repetition of Karma deepens the impression and desire to repeat it. When the samskaras become sufficiently deep, the action or thought becomes a habit and makes us good or bad, in spite of ourselves. Deeper the impressions, greater is the effort to change habit — it needs great will power, which everyone is not able to apply, unless trained to do it.

Jivatma — Mind as Bridge between Matter and Spirit

Living beings, Jivatmas, are "body", propelled by "Life". The body of a Jiva, which also includes its brain, is matter; it is inert. It is the presence of life, which is the Consciousness, which transforms the body into a living being through the subtle Mind and the Praana.

Not brain but Mind is our instrument of perception. When body-brain dies, the mind remains in a subtle form, carrying the impressions of all that the living being has experienced. Mind, however, is also matter and does not have consciousness, but the Mind reflects the consciousness of the "Spirit", Life, Self, "Kingdom of God" or Atman within all living beings, which alone has consciousness. Thus, the Mind is the subtlest matter, so subtle that it is all pervasive, not only within the living beings, but throughout the universe. Subtler than the Mind is only the one, omnipotent, omniscient, omnipresent God, the cause of the universe. Being so subtle and being in close proximity with the infinite Consciousness, the Mind seemingly borrows consciousness and enlivens the body, which is matter and acts as a bridge between matter and spirit.

Appendix 2

Brief on Different Types of Meditations

Referencess for different types of meditations:
- Preksha Dhyan www.preksha.com/
- Vipassana https://www.dhamma.org/en/about/vipassana
- Art of living www.artofliving.org/
- Sahaj Samadhi www.sahajayoga.org.in/
- Kriya yoga www.yogananda-srf.org/kriya_yoga_path_of_meditation.aspx
- Hong Sau www.yogananda.com.au/pyr/pyr_hong-sau.html
- Transcendental meditation https://www.tm.org/
- Japa meditation www.clear-mind-meditation-techniques.com/japa-mantra-meditation
- Buddhist breath meditation www.buddhanet.net/e-learning/qanda06.htm
- Zen meditation www.zen-buddhism.net/practice/zen-meditation.html
- Mindful meditation www.zen-buddhism.net/practice/zen-meditation.html
- Sahaj yoga meditation www.sahajayoga.org.in/

- Raj yoga or Ashtang yoga meditation: www.brahmakumaris.org/whatwedo/courses/fcirym www.sanatansociety.org › Yoga and Meditation › The Main Yoga Traditions
- Guided meditation
- Kabbalah meditation https://en.wikipedia.org/wiki/Jewish_meditation
- Heart centred meditation www.drweil.com/.../Heart-Center-Meditation-Dr-Ann-Marie-Chiasson.ht
- Mantra meditation https://www.artofliving.org/mantra-meditation
- Steady gaze meditation www.healthandyoga.com › ... › Meditation Articles › Trataka
- Chakra meditation www.wellbeingalignment.com/chakra-meditation.html
- Bahai's faith meditation www.bahai.org › What Bahá'ís Believe › The Life of the Spirit › Devotion
- Daoism meditation www.thewayofmeditation.com.au/blog/taoist-meditations/
- Soham meditation sivanandaonline.org › Meditation › Kinds of Meditation › Nirguna Meditation
- Sikh meditation https://kamallarosekaur.wordpress.com/.../practicing-the-sikh-way-naam
- Sufi meditation www.goldensufi.org/a_meditation_of_heart.html
- Yoga nidra meditation https://en.wikipedia.org/wiki/Yoga_nidra
- Coherence meditation www.heartmath.com/quick-coherence-technique/

Brief on different types of meditation

This list is illustrative and not exhaustive:

Preksha Dhyan

According to Jain Muni Shri Kishan Lal, Preksha is a meditative technique to awaken one's own disciplinary mind. For Preksha Dhyan, one has to sit, keeping the backbone upright and eyes shut gently.

The basic components of Preksha Meditation are:
- Kayotsarg (relaxation)
- Antaryatra (internal trip)
- Shvas Preksha (perception of breathing)
- Sharir Preksha (perception of physical body)
- Chaitanya Kendra Preksha (perception of psychic centres)
- Leshya Dhyna (perception of psychic colour)
- Anupreksha (contemplation)
- Chanting of Mantras (mantra meditation)

Select a calm and clean place for meditation and use a mat for sitting during meditation practice. There are four common sitting postures:
1. Lotus position (Padmaasan)
2. Half-lotus position (Ardha-padmaasan)
3. Simple cross-legged position (Sukhaasan)
4. Diamond position (Vajraasan)

The position of the hands (Mudra) is also very important:

Select a comfortable posture as described above. Close the eyes gently.

Recitation of ARHAM or Mahapraan Dhvani
Aphorism of Meditation Purpose (Dhyeya Sutra)
Resolve for meditation (Sankalp Sutra)

Technique

This meditation consists of four steps. In the first step, we try to get relaxed. In second step — Internal trip — we initiate upward movement of vital energy and awaken our supine power. The third step is perception of deep breathing and the fourth step is for attaining peace, pacifying anxieties and passions.

Step 1: Kayotsarg (5 mins)

Practice Kayotsarg to achieve stillness, relaxation and awareness. Take concentration to each part of body from toe of leg up to the head, one by one. Auto-suggest those parts to become relaxed and experience relaxation.

Step 2: Internal Trip (5 mins)

- Take your mind to the lower end of the spinal cord, called the Centre of Energy.
- Allow your mind to go upward inside your spinal cord up to the top of the head called the Centre of Knowledge.
- Again allow it to come back through the same path to the Centre of Energy.
- Again and again repeat the same process.
- Let your mind continuously undertake the trip inside the spinal cord and perceive the subtle vibrations of the vital energy, taking place inside the spinal cord, or whatever sensation you get there.
- Simply perceive them without any reaction. Concentrate your entire consciousness on the spinal cord.

You may synchronize your internal trip with the process of breathing. During exhalation, undertake the upward trip and during inhalation, undertake the downward trip. Use deep concentration and complete awareness.

Allow your mind to rise and fall inside the spinal cord just like mercury rising and falling inside the instrument used for measuring blood pressure.

Step 3: Perception of Deep Breathing

- Make the breath slow, long, and rhythmic.
- During inhalation, the abdominal muscles should expand.
- During exhalation, the abdominal muscles should contract.
- Let the vibrations of each breath reach your navel.
- Then perceive each inhalation and exhalation through the respiratory tract. While you are breathing in, let your attention follow the breath inside. While you are breathing out, let your attention follow it outside.
- Let your mind and breath go hand in hand. Continuously the mind and breath should accompany each other.
- Continuously practice slow, long and rhythmic breathing—inhale and exhale each breath while remaining fully aware of it.

Step 4: Perception of Bright White Colour on the Centre of Enlightenment (5 mins)

- Concentrate your mind on the Centre of Enlightenment, situated in the middle of your forehead.
- Allow your mind to penetrate inside and perceive bright white colour there. You may visualize as if the bright white light of the full moon is spreading throughout the portion or visualize the bright white colour of the snow or any other white thing.
- Practice concentrated visualization of bright white colour on the centre of enlightenment.
- Perceiving the bright white colour, experience through auto-suggestion that all your passions & emotions are

being pacified. All your excitations are subsiding. Your anger is waning away.
- Now allow your mind to spread throughout the whole portion of your forehead and perceive the bright white colour there.
- Visualize that the particles of bright white light are permeating the whole portion of the forehead, covering the emotional area in the frontal lobe of your brain.
- Continuously perceive bright white colour and experience complete tranquillity, complete mental peace and bliss.

Conclude with chanting of Vivek Sutra.

Vipassana

The technique of Vipassana is a simple, practical way to achieve real peace of mind and to lead a happy, useful life. Vipassana means "to see things as they really are". It is a logical process of mental purification through self-observation.

Vipassana is one of India's most ancient meditation techniques. It was rediscovered 2,500 years ago by Gautama Buddha. Over time, the technique spread to the neighbouring countries of Myanmar (Burma), Sri Lanka, Thailand and others.

Five centuries after the Buddha, the noble heritage of Vipassana had disappeared from India. However, it was preserved by a group of devoted teachers in Myanmar.

Vipassana has been reintroduced into India, as well as to citizens from more than 80 other countries, by S. N. Goenka. He was authorized to teach Vipassana by the renowned Burmese Vipassana teacher, Sayagyi U Ba Khin.

S. N. Goenka has trained over 800 assistant teachers who have conducted many courses worldwide. It has been taught to prisoners of Tihar Jail in New Delhi also.

The Practice

To learn Vipassana, it is necessary to take a ten-day residential course under the guidance of a qualified teacher. For the duration of the retreat, students remain within the course site, having no contact with the outside world. They refrain from reading and writing, and suspend any religious practices or other disciplines. They follow a demanding daily schedule, which includes about ten hours of sitting in meditation. They also observe silence, not communicating with fellow students. However, they are free to discuss meditation questions with the teacher and material problems with the management.

There are three steps to the training. First, the students practice abstinence from actions which cause harm. They undertake five moral precepts, practising abstention from killing, stealing, lying, sexual misconduct and the use of intoxicants. The observation of these precepts allows the mind to calm down sufficiently to proceed with the task at hand. Second, for the first three-and-a-half days, students practise Anapana meditation, focusing attention on the breath. This practise helps to develop control over the unruly mind.

Although Vipassana is a part of Buddha's teaching, it contains nothing of a sectarian nature and can be accepted and applied by people of any background.

Vipassana courses are open to anyone sincerely wishing to learn the technique, irrespective of race, caste, faith or nationality. Hindus, Jains, Muslims, Sikhs, Buddhists, Christians, Jews, as well as members of other religions have all successfully practiced Vipassana.

Art of Living

Meditation is that which gives you deep rest. - Ravi Shankar

The rest in meditation is deeper than the deepest sleep that you can ever have. When the mind becomes free from agitation, is calm and serene and at peace, meditation happens. Details of this method are not available in the open domain and one has to learn it by attending the programmes.

Sahaj Samadhi Meditation

Sahaj Samadhi Meditation is a mantra-based meditation where a sound vibration (mantra), when used in a specific way, gives you deep relaxation and also keeps you alert. It effortlessly allows the conscious mind to settle down. And when the mind settles down, it lets go of all tension and stress and centres itself in the present moment.

Everyone has experienced a meditative state in moments of deep joy, or when completely engrossed in an activity, when just for a moment the mind becomes so light and at ease. While we have such moments, we are unable to repeat them at will. The Sahaj Samadhi course teaches you how. This meditation technique almost instantly alleviates the practitioner from stress-related problems, deeply relaxes the mind and rejuvenates the system.

Sahaj is a Sanskrit word that means natural or effortless. *Samadhi* is a deep, blissful, meditative state. *Sahaj Samadhi meditation* is a natural, effortless system of meditation.

Regular practise of the technique can totally transform the quality of one's life, by culturing the system to maintain the peace, energy and expanded awareness throughout the day. These meditation techniques combined with yogic practices can ensure good health and a calm mind.

The participant is taught to use a simple sound mentally which allows the mind to settle down and go within. When the mind and nervous system are allowed to repose a few moments in the profound silence, the blocks that clog the system and our progress gradually dissolve.

Kriya Yoga Meditation

Around 1920, Paramahansa Yogananda introduced Kriya Yoga meditation to the West and founded the Self-Realization Fellowship. Kriya Yoga meditation refers to actions designed to get rid of obstructions involving body and mind. Kriya Yoga meditation is a complete system covering a wide range of techniques, including mantras and techniques of meditation for control of the life-force, bringing calmness and control of both body and mind. The goal is to unite with pure Awareness. Since pure Awareness is our original condition, it is also referred to as Self-awareness.

Kriya Yoga is said to be a combination of the more useful Yoga techniques. Like Raja Yoga, Kriya teaches the laws of general conduct, including harmlessness, truthfulness, non-stealing. The major components are:

1. Life-force control (pranayama): At this point, the difference from other systems, like Raja Yoga meditation, becomes quite obvious. Kriya pranayama is not as much about increasing the time of retention of breath but to magnetize the spine and direct life-force to the brain with the effect to refine the brain and nervous system.
2. Initiation and Shaktipat (transfer of energy): The seeker is initiated in the proper use of Kriya pranayama. When the seeker is ready, a transfer of energy might occur either from the outside or from within. To experience Kundalini (energy) on its way up the spine is an event powerful enough to change the way we think and function.
3. Higher Kriyas: For advanced students there are still a few higher Kriya meditation techniques. Full Self-realization may be achieved by practicing faithfully the Mantras given for regular Meditation.

Technique

- Sit upright with a straight spine, away from the back of the chair. Place your feet flat on the floor, and your arms, palms turned upward, at the joint between your thighs and torso.
- Do this Tense and Relax exercise to help you relax the body:
    - Inhale sharply through the nose, with 1 short and 1 long inhalation (double breath)
    - Tense the whole body until it vibrates with energy
    - Hold your breath and the tension for five seconds

- ▸ Exhale forcibly through the mouth, with one short and one long exhalation (double breath)
- ▸ As you do, throw the tension out
- Repeat several times
- Breathe evenly
- Inhale slowly, counting to eight. Hold the breath for eight more counts, then exhale slowly to the same count. Without pausing, inhale again—hold—exhale, each to the count of eight.

This is called the Measured Breathing Exercise and repeated three to six times.

You can vary the count according to your lung capacity, but always keep it *equal* during inhalation, holding, and exhalation. Finish your practice by inhaling deeply, then exhaling completely.

Hong-Sau Technique of Concentration

In this technique you wait for the next breath to come in of its own accord. When it does, mentally say *Hong* (rhymes with *song*). This time, don't hold the breath, but exhale naturally. As you do, mentally say *Sau* (rhymes with *saw*).

Hong-Sau is an ancient Sanskrit mantra (a *mantra* is a word, syllable, or group of syllables, which can convey spiritual power when pronounced correctly, often with repetition). It means "I am He" or "I am Spirit." Try to feel that your breath itself is silently making the sounds of Hong and Sau.

Meditation steps

Practicing the Tense and Relax exercise is an effective way to release stored-up bodily tension. Together with the Measured Breathing Exercise, these are preliminary exercises taught by Yogananda to help prepare the body and mind for meditation.

1. Pray

Begin your meditation with a prayer. This will help you remember why you are meditating! You will also be inviting the Divine, or your Higher Self, to help you in your practice.

2. Sit Perfectly Still

Moving your body even slightly sends the energy into the muscles. The purpose of yoga is to withdraw that energy inward and upward, to the brain. Thus, any physical movement during meditation will counteract your meditative effort.

3. Eye Position

Your eyes should be closed and held steady, looking slightly upwards, as if looking at a point about an arm's length away and level with the top of your head.

4. Do Not Control Your Breath

After the preliminary breathing exercises, you should cease any effort to control the breath. Let it flow naturally. You may notice that the pauses between the inhalation and exhalation are gradually becoming longer.

Enjoy these pauses, for they are a glimpse of the deep state of advanced meditation. As you grow very calm, your breath may become so shallow, and the pauses so prolonged, that it hardly seems necessary to breathe at all.

Two things, however, are essential: your spine must be straight, and you must be able to relax completely without slouching.

The material given above is a greatly abbreviated explanation of the Hong-Sau Technique of Concentration. The full instruction is available from *The Ananda Course in Self-Realization*.

Transcendental Meditation (TM)

Transcendental Meditation (TM) technique is a simple, natural, effortless procedure, practiced 20 minutes twice each day, while sitting comfortably with the eyes closed. It's not a religion, philosophy, or lifestyle. It is the most widely practised, most researched, and most effective method of self-development.

The Transcendental Meditation technique allows your mind to settle inward, beyond thought, to experience the source of thought — pure awareness, also known as transcendental consciousness. This is the most silent and peaceful level of consciousness — your innermost Self. In this state of restful alertness, your brain functions with significantly greater coherence and your body gains deep rest.

More than five million people worldwide have learned this simple, natural technique — people of all ages, cultures and religions. The Transcendental Meditation technique is based on the ancient Vedic tradition in India of enlightenment. This knowledge has been handed down by Vedic masters from generation to generation for thousands of years. About 50 years ago, Maharishi Mahesh Yogi introduced Transcendental Meditation to the world, restoring the knowledge and experience of higher states of consciousness at this critical time for humanity.

A large number of scientific studies on the benefits of meditation, which have been done in the West, are based on the practitioners of TM. It is reported to be one of the most widely practised and among the most widely researched meditation techniques, with over 340 peer-reviewed studies published. Beginning in 1965, the Transcendental Meditation technique has been incorporated into selected schools, universities, corporations and prison programs in the USA, Latin America, Europe and India. The Transcendental Meditation technique has been described as both religious and non-religious, as an aspect of a new religious movement, as rooted in Hinduism and as a non-religious practice for self-development. The public presentation of the TM technique over its 50-year history has been praised for its high visibility in the mass media and effective global propagation and criticized for using celebrity and scientific endorsements as a marketing tool.

Japa Meditation

Regarded as one of most effective ways of meditation, Japa Meditation helps sooth the mind and clears away the numerous impinging problems and worries that cloud it from time to time. Prevalent from ancient times, Japa Meditation has been in vogue and practised by all religions such as Hindus, Christians, Muslims and others to enable them to experience peace, calmness and tranquillity in their minds and life.

Meditation involves focusing the mind on a certain objective or thing or thought by shutting out the disturbing external stimuli. Meditation, or the peace of mind, can be achieved by different ways. One of the ways involves mental chanting or repetition of mantras to ease one's stress and tension.

Japa Meditation involves chanting of a mantra, which in most instances is composed of Sanskrit letters which are so arranged so as to evoke a certain response from within the individual. The vibrations of such mantras are extremely effective in creating a very significant change in attitudes and mind-sets of individuals. This helps in focusing one's energies so as to achieve a sense of calmness within oneself.

Mantras can also be any word which evokes a sense of calmness, inspiration and even respect, such as repeating the name of God, or anything else.

There are usually two ways in which individuals can practise Japa Meditation. One is audible Japa Meditation, also known as Vaikhari Japa, which includes repetition of mantras in whispers and even audible pitch. The other method is the silent or mental Japa Meditation which is also known as Manasika Japa. Manasika Japa is considered to be extremely powerful as it involves the complete focusing of the mind and hence, once achieved, it tends to obstruct any outside influences from disturbing the mind.

Usually the best ways in which one can practise Japa Meditation is by sitting cross-legged on a sheet or cloth on the ground and chant the mantra by beading the rosary of 108 beads with concentration, perseverance and dedication.

(Mantra meditation, with the use of a japa mala and especially with focus on the Hare Krishna Maha-mantra, is a central practice of the Gaudiya Vaishnava faith tradition and the International Society for Krishna Consciousness — ISKCON — also known as the Hare Krishna movement.)

Buddhist Breath Meditation

Buddhist meditation refers to the meditative practices associated with the religion and philosophy of Buddhism. Core meditation techniques have been preserved in ancient Buddhist texts and have proliferated and diversified through teacher-student transmissions. Buddhists pursue meditation as part of the path toward Enlightenment and Nirvana.

Buddhist meditation techniques have become increasingly popular in the wider world, with many non-Buddhists taking them up for a variety of reasons. There is considerable homogeneity across meditative practices — such as breath meditation and various recollections (anussati) — which are used across Buddhist schools, as well as significant diversity. In the Theravāda tradition alone, there are over 50 methods for developing mindfulness and 40 for developing concentration, while in the Tibetan tradition there are thousands of visualization meditations. Most classical and contemporary Buddhist meditation guides are school-specific.

Buddha is said to have identified two paramount mental qualities that arise from wholesome meditative practice:

- "serenity" or "tranquillity" (Pali: *samatha*) which steadies, composes, unifies and concentrates the mind;
- "insight" (Pali: *vipassana*) which enables one to see, explore and discern "formations" (conditioned phenomena based on the five aggregates).

The Dalai Lama has been acknowledged by Tibetan Buddhists to be a reincarnation of the God of Compassion. He is a Nobel Peace Prize winner, but few know him to be a practising meditator. All his life, he has been surrounded by masters of meditation and has been initiated into many different techniques. The technique advised by him is as follows:

- Sit quietly, calmly, with eyes closed, as relaxed yet aware as you can be. Visualize yourself on the left side of your mind's eye as you would appear to yourself and others in a moment of impatience. Really see this inner vision. Watch your face, observe your body language. What does your impatient self look like?

- On the right side of your mind's eye, see yourself when you are very patient. What do you look like when you have a lifetime of time? As tense as you appeared on the left as your impatient self, see yourself as relaxed in your patience on the right.

- Now on the left side, see yourself as you appear when you're depressed. Look carefully. How does that make you feel? Can you be aware of the aura of doom and gloom you're radiating? And then, on the right side of your mind's eye, see yourself as you are when you're joyous. Merge with that happiness. Know how others would see you.

- Continue seeing all the seemingly negative feelings and behaviours on the inner left-hand side of your mind's eye and the opposite on the right. On the left, see yourself as jealous and on the right as how you appear when you are truly glad for someone else's success or happiness. On the left, see the bigoted you and on the right, the all-embracing. On the left the mean, on the right the sweet. See the stupid you and the brilliant. See the clumsy and the graceful. On the left, see the unsatisfied and on the right, the contented.

- Go on and on, becoming familiar with the "you" on the left and the opposite "you" on the right. Then see the total "you" who would be there on the left if none of the characteristics of the right side were present. Now see the "you" who would be the totality of yourself with the right side only if none of the behaviours and feelings of the left side "you" had ever appeared.

Seven Steps of Classical Buddhists meditation are
Start out with three or seven long in-and-out breaths, thinking *bud* with the in-breath and *dho* with the out. Keep the meditation syllable as long as the breath.

Be clearly aware of each in-and-out breath during this meditation.

Observe the breath as it goes in and out, noticing whether it's comfortable or uncomfortable, broad or narrow, obstructed or free-flowing, fast or slow, short or long, warm or cool. If the breath doesn't feel comfortable, change it until it does.

To begin with, inhale the breath sensation at the base of the skull and let it flow all the way down the spine. Then, if you are male, let it spread down your right leg to the sole of your foot, to the ends of your toes, and out into the air. Inhale the breath sensation at the base of the skull again and let it spread down your spine, down your left leg to the ends of your toes and out into the air. (If you are female, begin with the left side first, because the male and female nervous systems are different.)

Then let the breath from the base of the skull spread down over both shoulders, past your elbows and wrists, to the tips of your fingers and out into the air.

Let the breath at the base of the throat spread down the central nerve at the front of the body, past the lungs and liver, all the way down to the bladder and colon.

Inhale the breath right at the middle of the chest and let it go all the way down to your intestines.

Let all these breath sensations spread so that they connect and flow together, and you'll feel a greatly improved sense of well-being.

Learn four ways of adjusting the breath:
a. in long and out long
b. in short and out short,
c. in short and out long,
d. in long and out short.

Breathe whichever way is most comfortable for you. Or, better still, learn to breathe comfortably all four ways, because your physical condition and your breath are always changing.

Become acquainted with the bases or focal points of the mind — the resting spots of the breath — and centre your awareness on whichever one seems most comfortable. A few of these bases are:
a. the tip of the nose,
b. the middle of the head,
c. the palate,
d. the base of the throat,
e. the breastbone (the tip of the sternum),
f. the navel (or a point just above it).

Let the mind be at ease with the breath — but not to the point where it slips away.

Spread your awareness–your sense of conscious feeling — throughout the entire body.

Coordinate the breath sensations throughout the body, letting them flow together comfortably, keeping your awareness as broad as possible.

Zen Meditation

Do not pursue the past.
Do not lose yourself in the future.
The past no longer is.

The future has not yet come.
Looking deeply at the life as it is
In the very here and now.
The practitioner dwells
in stability and freedom.
We must be diligent today,
to wait until tomorrow is too late.
Death comes unexpectedly.
How can we bargain with it?
The sage call a person who knows.
How to dwell in mindfulness
night and day.
"One who knows the better way to live alone?"
Our appointment with life
is in the present moment.
The place of our appointment is right here in this very place.

Reference: *Zen Speaks* by Tsai Chih Chung (Harper Collins, 1994) Buddha: Knowing the better way to live alone (Reference — The Sutra on knowing the better way to live alone — *Badder karatta Sutra*, translated by Thich Nhat Hanh in his book *Our appointment with life* Parallax Press, Berkley, California, 1990

Zen meditation allows the mind to relax. The steps are:
- Sit on the forward third of a chair or a cushion on the floor.
- Arrange your legs in a position you can maintain comfortably. In the half-lotus position, place your right leg on your left thigh.

In the full lotus position, put your feet on opposite thighs. You may also sit simply with your legs tucked in close to your body, but be sure that your weight is distributed on three points: both of your knees on the ground and your buttocks on the round cushion. On a chair, keep your knees apart about the width of your shoulders, feet firmly planted on the floor.

- Take a deep breath, exhale fully, and take another deep breath, exhaling fully.

- With proper physical posture, your breathing will flow naturally into your lower abdomen. Breathe naturally, without judgement or trying to breathe a certain way.
- Keep your attention on your breath whilst practicing Zen meditation. When your attention wanders, bring it back to the breath again and again—as many times as necessary! Remain as still as possible, following your breath and returning to it whenever thoughts arise.
- Be fully, vitally present with yourself. Simply do your very best. At the end of your sitting period, gently swing your body from right to left in increasing arcs. Stretch out your legs, and be sure they have feeling before standing.
- Zen meditation is recommended every day for at least 10 to 15 minutes (or longer).

Mindfulness Meditation

- The purpose of Mindful meditation is to deal with stressful situations by accepting them and being aware of them. It is an effective technique of meditation against life's problems and situations.
- Stress, anger, disappointments, frustrations, and other negative emotions adversely affect our minds and even bodies. Such negative emotions and actions should be dealt with effectively and setbacks should be accepted without injuring our health. Mindfulness Meditation is that medicine which helps to deal with negative emotions and situations in the most effective manner.
- Mindfulness Meditation, also referred to as Insightful Meditation, requires or allows individuals to be aware of their surroundings to develop a sense of sensitivity in perceiving every moment and enabling them to accept stressful situations, instead of avoiding them. By being aware of the inner state of our minds

during Mindfulness Meditation, we can accept difficult situations in our lives without much resistance.
- Through the practice of Mindfulness Meditation, we can train our minds to achieve a state of tranquillity, without being disturbed by outside forces. Mindfulness Meditation helps in training and developing the strengths of the mind to achieve this peacefulness.
- We can practice Mindfulness Meditation by sitting in an appropriate upright position, cross-legged and focusing on our breath or anything else, such as mental and physical processes which help us in becoming aware of our present thought patterns and inner state.
- The practice of Mindfulness Meditation focuses our attention on our thoughts, actions and present moments non-judgmentally. It does not encourage evaluating or thinking on our past actions and neither does it take our thoughts to the uncertain future. Mindfulness Meditation helps and trains our mind from getting distracted by outside disturbances and enables us to focus our thoughts and relax the mind.
- Mindfulness Meditation can be conducted or practised through informal and formal techniques. While formal Mindfulness Meditation involves Yoga, in which there is a control and awareness of breathing patterns with appropriate body movements, informal Mindfulness Meditation includes taking into account each experience in life with relish and enjoyment.

Descartes Meditation

A masterpiece created in 1641 by philosopher and scholar Rene Descartes, Descartes Meditation is a philosophical piece or treatise which expounds Descartes' opinions and thoughts on meta-physical system and philosophy.

Owing to its popularity and in-depth philosophical analysis, Descartes Meditation, written in Latin originally, was translated into French in 1647 and consequently, into English. Composed of six parts, otherwise called "meditations", Descartes Meditation describes in detail the philosophical thoughts and principles of Rene Descartes.

In the *first piece of Descartes Meditation*, Descartes attempts to re analyze the beliefs he has held since his childhood in order to establish truth in science. He forms a sceptical belief or hypotheses about everything in the physical world and decides to suspend his theory or judgement on his previously held beliefs.

In the *second part of Descartes Meditation*, which expounds Descartes theory on the "nature of human mind", Descartes questions his identity, the eternal "I", introduces a theory of representationalism and lays down the thought that "one's consciousness implies one's existence".

Descartes, in his *third part of Descartes Meditation*, discusses that there are three main categories of thoughts:
- volitions
- affections and
- judgements

and propounds that there are two main cause and effect relationships within classes of thought. He states that the *two cause and effect relationship* within such classes of thought include:
- whether our thoughts do not deceive us or
- whether we are deceived by our thoughts

Furthermore, Descartes, after analysis of such aforementioned classes of thought, also *establishes the existence of* "I" *and God.*

In the *fourth part of Descartes Meditation*, which is also known as the meditation "*on truth and falsity*", Descartes raises the question that if God, who is perfect, is the source of all on earth, then why is there falsehood or wrong doings in this world. Analysing his theories, Descartes realises that although God is perfect and has given him a special ability to judge, still his power of judgement, especially of the truth, is not infinite.

In the *fifth part of Descartes Meditation*, Descartes proposes that his knowledge about truth and everything else comes from God.

In the *sixth part of Descartes Meditation*, Descartes holds that there are other objects and materials which exist outside our *self* and recognizes the distinction between mind and body. He concludes by establishing the identity and existence of three things: *self, God, and other material objects*. According to Descartes, these three things make up what we call *reality*.

Sahaja Yoga Meditation

Sahaja Yoga is a meditation technique which brings a breakthrough in the transformation of human awareness. It was created by Shri Mataji Nirmala Devi in 1970 and has, since, spread all around the world.

Through the practice of **Sahaja Yoga meditation**, our awareness gains a new dimension, where absolute truth can be felt tangibly on our central nervous system. As a result of this happening, our spiritual ascent takes place effortlessly and physical, mental and emotional balance is achieved as a by-product of this growth of our awareness.

We then realize that we are not this body, mind, ego, conditionings, emotions or intellect, but something of an eternal nature which is always residing in our heart in a pure, undisturbed state—the Self or Spirit.

To learn more about Sahaja Yoga meditation please visit their website at:

http://www.freemeditation.com

Raja Yoga Meditation

Raja Yoga meditation has a foundation of the soul being a point of light and all meditations are based on this concept. Raja yoga literally means kingly yoga. It is a form of meditation which is based on relating a person's life to different ideas. It brings together the inner thoughts of the mind and emotions. It balances the attention on these aspects in order to provide a focused mind for meditation. Raja yoga uses a life force which moves from the upper body through the spine up to the lower body.

This type of yoga aims to balance the mind and emotions in a peaceful way. A person practising this meditation will be aware of the energy present in the mind and body. The person must be very calm and attempt to make his or her mind to be passive. It involves releasing meaningless worries, stresses and thoughts of the subconscious mind. At the end of every meditation in Raga Yoga, the person is expected to discover a pleasant sense of well-being. This sense fills the mind with free thoughts and thus gives him or her comfort to use the new thoughts freely.

Raja Yoga is also called as Classical Ashtang Yoga. Traditionally, there are eight aspects to which a person should be able to take into consideration. These eight aspects are as follows:

Ashtang yoga

According to Patanjali (the great ancient exponent of Raja Yoga), Yoga consists of the following eight limbs.

The first five are called external aids to Yoga (*bahiranga sadhana*).The last three levels are called internal aids to Yoga (*antaranga sadhana*).

1. The rules of Yama (the Don'ts) are five:
   - Non-violence or Ahimsa
   - Non-lying
   - Non-stealing
   - Non-sensuality or Brahmacharya
   - Non-greed or Non-attachment

2. The rules of Niyama (the Do's) are:
   - Cleanliness
   - Contentment
   - Austerity
   - Self-study or Introspection
   - Devotion to the Supreme Lord
3. *Asana* means, simply, posture. Posture means no particular set of postures, but only the ability to hold the body still as a prerequisite for deep meditation. Any comfortable posture will do, as long as the spine is kept erect and the body relaxed. Until the body can be mastered, higher perceptions, so subtle that they blossom only in perfect quiet, can never be achieved. It is good to practice some of the yoga postures before meditation. These postures help one to attain Asana, or firm posture.
4. *Pranayama*: *Prana* does mean breath, but only because of the close connection that exists between the breath and the causative flow of energy in the body. The word *prana* refers primarily to the energy itself. *Pranayama*, then, means energy control. This energy control is often affected with the aid of breathing exercises. Hence, breathing exercises have also come to be known as *Pranayama*. Patanjali's reference is to the energy control that is achieved as a result of various techniques and not to the techniques themselves. To direct this energy inwardly is the first step in divine contemplation.
5. *Pratyahara* means the internalization of the mind. Once the energy has been redirected towards its source in the brain, the person must then internalize his consciousness, so that his thoughts, too, will not wander in endless paths of restlessness and delusion, but will be focused single-pointedly on the deeper mysteries of the indwelling soul.
6. *Dharana* means contemplation, or fixed inner awareness. A person may have been aware of inner spiritual realities — the inner light, for instance, or the inner sound,

or deep mystical feelings—before reaching this stage, but it is only after reaching it that he can give himself completely to deep concentration on those realities.
7. *Dhyana* means meditation, absorption, steadfast meditation, undisturbed flow of thought around the object of meditation (*pratyayaikatanata*). The act of meditation and the object of meditation remain distinct and separate. By concentrating on the inner light, then, or upon any other divine reality that a person actually perceives when the mind is calm, he gradually takes on the qualities of that inner reality. The mind loses its ego identification and begins to merge in the great ocean of consciousness of which it is a part.
8. *Samadhi*: The eighth and final step on Patanjali's eightfold journey is known as *Samadhi*, i.e., oneness. *Samadhi* comes after a person learns to dissolve his ego consciousness in the calm inner light. Once the grip of ego has really been broken and the person discovers that he is that light, there is nothing to prevent him from expanding his consciousness to infinity. The devotee in deep Samadhi realizes the truth.

Raja Yoga is concerned with focusing the mind and using its power to control the body. Mind is perceived to be the king or controller of the person.

The basis for attaining an experience in Raja Yoga meditation is to understand the self and the mind. Using this energy called mind we have been able to search the deepest oceans, send humans to the moon and scan the molecular fabric of the building blocks of nature. But have we found our true self? We have become the most educated and civilized society in our history, but are we civil towards one another?

According to Raja Yoga meditation, the soul has three main faculties—the mind or consciousness, the intellect and the subconscious.

Thoughts flow from the sub conscious mind to the conscious mind. Feelings and emotions form in accordance with the montage of thoughts flowing in the mind. Therefore our state of mind at any given moment is determined by the thoughts in our consciousness and also with the feelings that we associate with those thoughts. Since our sub consciousness contains all our previous thoughts and experiences, it is necessary to selectively control the flow of thoughts that emerges from the subconscious mind.

The intellect is the controller which is used to discriminate so that only positive and benevolent thoughts flow into our mind. With meditation or deep contemplation, the individual is able to strengthen and sharpen the intellect. The end result is a constant state of well-being. If we are able to understand the self as the source of energy that creates our feelings, then the following will become our aims.

Become aware of our state of mind and of the thoughts that flows into the mind from our subconscious.

Strengthen the intellect so that the individual can discriminate and thereby only allow positive and peaceful thoughts to flow into the mind.

Through this process of self-development the individual develops more control over the mind.

Guided Meditation

Although there is no substitute for doing guided meditation in the presence of a guru or a master, it is quite often not possible to find an accomplished teacher in your close vicinity. The other alternative is to watch the videos or listen to audios of the guided meditation prepared by the realized masters.

Guided meditation means that the teacher guides your thought process, which you follow, like listening to your teachers in your schools and colleges.

While the meditation teacher is speaking, he is, in fact, taking you along on a journey of a whole new beautiful and blissful world, which is altogether different from this world. Although he may build up and correlate his theme of meditation with this world, he may suggest a line of refreshing and powerful thought process. The effect of meditation, guided by a realized master, will appear like a fresh, pure and blissful lotus emerging out of slush and mud of negative thoughts and mundane tensions.

The language may start in first person:
I am a spiritual being.
I am able to relax my mind.
I am a positive, blissful and compassionate soul.
I take charge of my thoughts and feelings to only allow peaceful thoughts and feelings of peace.

These or similar positive affirmations are repeated almost on daily basis till they become an integral part of our thought process.

Kabbalah Meditation

Kabbalah meditations were devised by Jewish mystics over 2,000 years ago to enhance the awareness and access higher planes of consciousness. The aim of Kabbalah meditation is to make the practitioners the true carriers of the light of God. Kabbalah meditation continues to flourish in the oral tradition and rises above the written word. This system will enable you to attain peace and happiness through union with God.

The objective of Kabbalah meditation transcends the need for relaxation and quieting the mind. Kabbalah meditation enables the seekers to directly interact with the higher worlds and bring about positive changes in life. It wipes off the negative influences both from your body and mind and establishes the power of mind over matter. The essence of Kabbalah meditation is to bring new sources of joy, love and understanding to everything you do.

Kabbalah meditation explores the complex character of the divine reality, particularly the inability of the human thought to grasp God. It uses various techniques, including meditations on Hebrew letter, permutations and combinations and the ways in which sefirot or the supernatural forces harmonize and interact with one another. These meditative techniques produce visionary experiences of the angels and their residential chambers. Another important objective of Kabbalah is to rectify the imperfections of the soul rather than creating spiritual knowledge.

Heart Centred Meditation

Begin by finding a quiet spot where you will not be disturbed. The major steps are as follows:

- Sit or lie down in a comfortable position. This could be on the floor, cross legged with back straight and hands resting on knees, palms facing upward and thumb and first finger held together in the traditional meditation position (you can rest against a wall if you like), or in an arm chair with back straight, feet flat on the ground and hands resting on thighs with palms flat. If you choose to lie down, this can be either on the ground with feet shoulder width apart, back straight and hands resting gently to the sides, or on a bed in the same position.

- Close your eyes. Take a deep breath, hold it in and tense up every muscle you can. Exhale and release the tension.

- Repeat this twice more, making it three breath/tensions in total.

- Visualize your muscles becoming relaxed and saturated with a brilliant, white light.

- Start at your toes and work your way up to the top of your head, pay particular attention to the shoulders, jaw and facial area, and any other area that may be causing you particular concern. All the while taking gentle, deep breaths.

- If you hear sounds such as cars passing by, people talking, dogs barking, etc., just let these sounds pass over you. Do not judge these sounds, simply allow them to occur and fade away, all the while taking gentle deep breaths.

- When you feel sufficiently relaxed, draw your attention to your chest area, and visualize a tiny ball of light that rests half inside and half outside the centre of your chest.
- This ball of light can be any colour that feels comfortable to you. I personally use the colour pink or blue flecked with brilliant gold. This ball of light starts out tiny, but expands gradually with every inhalation and every exhalation.
- Continue to visualize for this meditation so that the ball grows larger and larger, all the while producing a greater feeling of loving peace and calm.
- Allow the ball of light to grow as large as you feel comfortable with.
- This ball is a ball of healing love-energy. Allow the ball to move to wherever you need healing in your body.
- You can direct the ball or allow it to move by itself. If you have a loved one that needs healing or love, who may be emotionally troubled, you can send this ball of love-energy to this person in your mind.
- Visualize the ball leaving the room and travelling to the person in need. Or you can allow the ball to leave of its own accord; it will travel to someone who needs your love-energy. Or you can simply reabsorb the ball back into your body.

When you feel that the meditation has finished, gradually and gently bring your attention back to your surroundings and slowly open your eyes.

Mantra Meditation

Mantra, literally meaning "revealed sound", means a sound or combination of sounds which develop spontaneously. In mantra meditation, specific sounds are repeated (japa) to achieve a meditative state.

Appendix 2

- A Mantra is a grouping of sound vibrations which have an effect on the mental and psychic consciousness. Although traditionally given by a Guru, in the absence of a Guru, the practitioner may choose his mantra. An important criterion for mantra selection is that it must appeal to the mind fully when spoken verbally.

- Mantra chanting creates powerful vibrations which are said to be directed to the right "chakras" to attract divine forces. This process is said to mysteriously heal the spiritual, physical and psychological body. It is important that when the mantra is chanted, the words and their rhythm must be enjoyed and the person must surrender himself to this experience.

- Mantras do not have any specific meaning. Their power lies not in the meaning of the word but through the vibratory effects of the sound that they produce when spoken verbally or mentally.

- Repetition of a Mantra forms the basis of Mantra Meditation. Mantras for spiritual evolution should be practiced for a fixed amount of time each day. Repeating a mantra too much may not be right for sensitive or psychic people as it may affect them adversely. Generally, if you repeat a mantra for about 10 minutes every day, then, within a few days you will know whether the vibrations feel right for you.

- Transcendental Meditation (TM) introduced by Maharishi Mahesh Yogi is also a form of Mantra Meditation where the participants are provided their personal Mantra.

- Mantra Meditation is the easiest and safest form of meditation and can be practised by anyone at any time and under any conditions. The most common way of practicing Mantra Meditation is Japa. Japa (literally meaning "rotate") is performed by repeating a mantra in sync with the rotation of a Japa Mala. A Japa Mala is a rosary of 108 beads where each bead is turned after the mental or audible recitation of the mantra.

- Using a Japa Mala for Mantra Meditation is very effective as it provides an anchor to bring the mind back as soon as it experiences wavering thoughts. The Mantra, combined with the Japa Mala, provides tangible anchors to which the thoughts are directed back whenever they spin out of control. That is why Japa Meditation is one of the most recommended forms of meditation for the beginner.

Steady Gaze (Trataka)

Trataka (to gaze steadily) has been followed by most religious systems, including Christianity and Sufism. In Trataka, a steady gaze is performed on an object. While it strictly comes under the category of a yoga cleansing technique, effective Trataka practice takes one to the shores of meditation.

Method:

- In this a regular candle is used, however any other object of choice can be used. The candle is set up at an arm's distance, level with the eyes and steady gazing is first done with the eyes open.
- After some time, the eyes are closed and the after-image of the flame is "gazed at" with eyes closed, at the eyebrow centre.
- Try not to move throughout the practice. Relax your breath, let it lengthen, deepen.

This open gazing of the flame and then with the eyes closed is alternated a couple of times before concluding the practice.

If using a candle for *Trataka*, the gaze should be fixed at the wick tip and not on the flame.

Trataka on a candle flame is best practised with a Trataka stand.

Benefits:

- It improves the optic function, both external and internal, such as poor eyesight and visualization abilities.
- It helps develop concentration and mental resolve.
- It develops the ability to maintain single-pointedness among the noise and distractions of daily life.
- It develops the psychic eye, that is, the ability to "see" or understand what is inside and beyond the obvious. It develops the power of Intuition.

This open gazing of the flame and then with the eyes closed is alternated a couple of times before concluding the practice. Caution: If practising Trataka on a candle flame, do not continue the practice for more than a month or two at a stretch as it may lead to damage of the retina.

Chakras Meditation

Chakras means *wheel* and represent the major nerve plexi which branch off the spinal cord to serve the major organs of the body. Chakras represent a different level of energy manifestation and consciousness development. There are 7 Chakras.

Chakra Anusandhana means *discovery or search of the chakras*. It is a simple way for beginners to explore the chakras, self-tutored. It helps in awakening them gently and in a balanced integrated way.

Modalities for meditation:
- It can be done sitting or lying down.
- Close your eyes, adjust your body and clothing.
- Let the breath relax, slow and deepen, but do not control it.
- After a few minutes of settling in, commence Ujjayi pranayam and carry on for some time.

- Now bring awareness to the spinal passage, such that the *awareness of breath is from bottom to top*. Spend a few minutes establishing this inner breath pattern up and down. Ascending with inhalation, descending with exhalation.
- Begin to locate chakras within that channel. You need not pin point the exact location, just focus on the general area. Try to feel the location of each station and mentally repeat its name as you pass by it. On your way up, mentally repeat from Mooldhara to Ajna and on the way down, in the reverse the order.
- Just before finishing, let go of breath sound, then names. And chant the mantra "Om" three times.

Precaution:

- Awakening of Chakra can have its side effects. Excessive mental energy can be a problem with those who do not have abundant physical activity.
- Never meditate on one Chakra without qualified guidance. It can lead to an imbalance and cause personality problems.

Meditation is an intensely personal and spiritual experience with positive direction by totally transforming one's state of mind.

Bahá'í Faith meditation

In the teachings of the Bahá'í Faith, meditation, along with prayer, is one of the primary tools for spiritual development and it mainly refers to a person's reflection on the words of God. While prayer and meditation are linked, where meditation happens generally in a prayerful attitude, prayer is seen specifically as turning toward God and meditation is seen as a communion with our self where we focuses on the divine.

The Bahá'í teachings note that the purpose of meditation is to strengthen our understanding of the words of God, and to make our soul more susceptible to their potentially transformative power and that both prayer and meditation are needed to bring about and to maintain a spiritual communion with God.

Bahá'u'lláh, the founder of the religion, never specified any particular form of meditation and thus each person is free to choose their own form. However, he specifically did state that Bahá'ís should read a passage of the Bahá'í writings twice a day, once in the morning and once in the evening and meditate on it. He also encouraged people to reflect on their actions and worth at the end of each day. The Nineteen Day Fast, a nineteen-day period of the year during which Bahá'ís adhere to a sunrise-to-sunset fast, is also seen as meditative, where Bahá'ís must meditate and pray to reinvigorate their spiritual forces.

Daoism (Taoist meditation)

Taoist or Daoist meditation has a long history and has developed various techniques including concentration, visualization, qi cultivation, contemplation and mindfulness meditations. Traditional Daoist meditative practices were influenced by Chinese Buddhism, beginning around the 5th century and later had influence upon Traditional Chinese medicine and the Chinese martial arts.

Livia Kohn distinguishes three basic types of Daoist meditation:
- concentrative,
- insight, and
- visualization

It was developed by Tang Dynasty (618–907) Daoist masters, based upon the Tiantai Buddhist practice of Vipassana insight or wisdom meditation.

It has a sense of "to cause to exist; to make present" in the meditation techniques popularized by the Daoist Shangqing and Lingbao Schools.

A meditator visualizes or actualizes solar and lunar essences, lights and deities within his or her body, which supposedly results in health and longevity, even "immortality".

"When you enlarge your mind and let go of it, when you relax your vital breath and expand it, when your body is calm and unmoving; And you can maintain the One and discard the myriad disturbances... This is called 'revolving the vital breath': Your thoughts and deeds seem heavenly."

Daoist meditation practices are central to Chinese martial arts (and some Japanese martial arts), especially the qi related Neijia "internal martial arts". Some well-known examples are Daoyin "guiding and pulling", Qigong "life-energy exercises", Neigong "internal exercises", Neidan "internal alchemy" and Taijiquan "great ultimate boxing", which is thought of as moving meditation.

- Don't dwell on the past.
- Don't worry about the future.
- Experience and cherish the moment.
- Happiness is acting according to the circumstances, whatever they may be.
- We all experience troubles and worries, but it often happens that our greatest troubles arise from ourselves.
- How many people wake up in the morning still figuring out problems from the day before? We should take everything that threatens our peace of mind and throw it out. We should live according to our original nature because the ordinary mind is the DAO.

Sham Meditation

It is referred to as the Mahamantra, the Greatest Mantra, and is considered along with Om to be the most powerful of all techniques. This was the first meditation technique, both in antiquity and in our own lives. The ancient cavemen, before they had invented language or fire, would sit in their dark caves and have nothing else to focus on but the sound of their breath. Similarly, the first sound we heard when we were in our mothers' womb was the sound of her breath and this sound has been with us ever since we drew our first breath. It negates the need to rely on any of the words of the languages of the world to use as a mantra. It has brought people to transcendence of worldly limitations from time immemorial and continues to do so. It can be done even while driving, working and doing other acts of daily life and thereby offers a continuous experience of being in the present. This is a great present, because Reality takes place now, in the present. Soham is a wonderful meditation technique and I hope it will bring you the experience of Knowledge, Consciousness and Bliss that is your birth right.

In Sanskrit, the most ancient of languages, the sound of the inhalation is termed So, and the exhalation is Ham. Combined, the word Soham is translated as "I Am He/That". So, whenever you are doing this technique, you are calling on God. Every breath thus becomes a prayer and adoration.

The Soham Meditation Technique

At the time and in the place where you feel most comfortable, place your body in the position that you have found to be the most beneficial for meditation. Close your eyes. Close your ears by putting your thumbs in them, or by using earplugs. This will intensify the sound of your breath, while diminishing the distractions that sight and sound bring. Command your mind to be silent, your emotions to be calm and your body to stay relaxed. Focus on the sound of your breath coming in. Associate it with the word So. As your breath leaves, listen to the sound and associate it with the word Ham. To pronounce So and Ham correctly, listen to how they sound. As with most pranayama (breathing techniques),

Soham is done either in 3 cycles of 12 or 12 cycles of 12. One inhalation and one exhalation are one respiration. And 12 respirations are one cycle. For those just starting to use this technique, it is usual to silently say the word So with each inhalation and the word Ham with each exhalation. When you are focused consistently, consciously, you will flow into simply listening to the sound of Soham. Soham is by far the easiest meditation. It comes to all living creatures without any effort. And yet it is the deepest possible technique, as it presents the opportunity to meditate on the great mystery of life and the life-giver itself.

No matter how we have acted and reacted, with each breath we are forgiven for our so-called sins and rewarded with another breath, another heartbeat and another moment of life to cherish. No act of will on our part can give us breath. Literally, we are graced with this gift of life from a power greater than ourselves. A corpse has every bone, every organ and every bodily system that we have, and yet it doesn't have life or healing energy filling every cell with every breath, as we have. As you merge more and more with Soham, you surrender your reactivity to your thoughts, emotions and sensory impressions. These are all just heavy earth-bound suffering-causing limitations. The divine energy of Soham is limitless heavenly love and light. Witness, surrender all effort and fill with this most precious gift of Grace.

Sikh Meditation

Naam Jape is the recital of the name of God (Naam) or the repetition of sacred verses written in the Guru Granth Sahib, the Sikh sacred text. This has particular significance due to the fact that Sikhs consider the Guru Granth Sahib to be a living prophet in text form, notated especially for musical recital. These hymns lend themselves to practise and repetition in such a way as to make meditation a central pillar of Sikh practice and were handed to all Sikhs by the tenth living human Guru's Guru Gobind Singh as a final guru that will continuously guide its followers.

Appendix 2

Naam Jaap, the practice of invoking the Name of the Beloved One, is practised by Sikhs to cure dualistic perception and to invite the Cosmic One into each moment.

1. Jaap

Jaap means recitation. It is repeating the name of God. It may be verbal or mental. We start with verbal Jaap and develop it into the mental Jaap. Verbal Jaap is the starting or gross stage of Jaap. In it, there is so called a perceptible Naam (perceptible name of God — you know you are reciting it).

2. Ajappaa-Jaap

Ajapaa-Jaap is a Jaap (recitation) without doing Jaap. In this, recitation of the name of God (Jaap) becomes a habit. It is a Jaap without effort — an effortless Jaap. The Jaap of the Name (Naam — name of God) keeps going on verbally, or silently in the mind. Whatever might a person be doing, the act of Jaap is there. The constant Jaap leads to Ajapaa-Jaap. This is the middle, i.e., subtle stage of Jaap — imperceptible Naam: the recitation becomes automatic, like a habit.

3. Simran

Simran is remembrance. The mind gets filled with the constant remembrance of the One, and there is no more recitation of the Naam (Waheguru). Only the remembrance of the Divine One is left — an unbroken awareness of the Infinite One. God is always in the mind, regardless of what the person might be busy with. It is an advanced stage of the seeker-practitioner (the person reciting the Naam). It is the third, i.e., transcendental stage of the Jaap. This is the Naam beyond perception (recitation without knowing it — Just the thought).

4. Dheaan

Dheaan is meditation — contemplation on the Beloved One. It is thinking about God and is different from Jaap — recitation of the Naam. Dheaan is the process of thinking about God and may include changing thoughts.

In the Naam-Jaap, there is recitation of the name of the Divine One and it stays the same without any change. The mind keeps set on God. The mind is set on the Name as it is, without its modification—no changing thoughts, no thinking about various aspects of the Name.

Naam—Waheguru

Naam is the Gurmantar—formula given by the Guru, and for the Sikhs it is the word Waheguru. It means, "the wonderful one who removes ignorance", i.e., the giver of the light of God—Divine knowledge. It is also called Shabad or Word. The word Waheguru is not combined with any other word and Sikhs use it exclusively to do Jaap. For Sikhs, only the word Waheguru is the Naam. The pure Naam-Jaap is recitation only of the word Waheguru. In the Sikh world, Naam-Jaap pertains to recitation of the word Waheguru.

According to the occasion and need, instructions are modified. The sequence of different steps and their contents may as well get affected in order to simplify the subject in an effort to make it easily understandable and applicable.

Preliminaries

Every technique of the Naam Jaap is nothing but an effort to achieve concentration on recitation of the Naam—Waheguru. Practice of the Naam

Stage I

You may start with vocally reciting Waheguru, Waheguru, without any restraint or inhibition. It may be with or without a Mala (rosary), or a musical instrument. Gradually, recitation will be done without any Mala, or instrument, and ultimately it will become mental, without making any sound.

Stage II

Sit down properly, according to your convenience. Do the Jaap of Waheguru, speaking out the Word (loudly), hearing the voice, and concentrating on it. In the background, God is always there in the mind. When well practised, go to the next step.

Sit down properly. Do Jaap of Waheguru in a whisper, lightly focusing both eyes at the tip of the nose. When practised, close your eyes when focusing. Try to hear your whisper, concentrate on the whispered word Waheguru, and keep God in the mind. When well practised, move to the next step. Whenever focusing eyes at any point, do so free from stress and strain on them and turn them in very lightly. Turning eyes in too much and with strain, will lead to a headache.

Sit down properly. Do the silent Jaap of the Naam Waheguru at the level of your throat (in the throat).

If you can, concentrate on the imaginary sound of the word Waheguru. Focus your closed eyes at the bridge of your nose (where the bridge of glasses stays normally). When well practised, move to the next step.

Stage III

Silent Jaap of Waheguru. Recite Waheguru in your heart (mentally), without making any sound.
Concentrate on the Shabad (Word) Waheguru, and its imaginary sound.
Focus your closed eyes on the space between your two eyebrows, and slightly higher up — mid-brow Point.
Link the Jaap to breathing:
When inhaling – breathing in, mentally say Wahe.
When exhaling – breathing out, mentally say Guru.
To clarify any point regarding the Naam Jaap, it is best to consult some local Naam practicing Gurmukh (God-oriented person).

Sufi Meditation

The Sufi meditation technique uses practices traditionally known as zikr, common to most Sufi tariqas—chants, hymns and ritual movements that date back centuries. While the forms of Sufi meditation technique have a religious context and expression, no belief is asked for in Sufi meditation technique practise—only heartfelt, ecstatic practice itself is required.

Sufi meditation is a mystic tradition of Islam encompassing a diverse range of beliefs. Sufi meditation technique practices dedicated to the love and service of our fellow men and Allah or God. Tariqas (Sufi orders) may be associated with Shi'a Islam, Sunni Islam, other currents of Islam, or a combination of multiple traditions.

Sufi meditation is generally reckoned to originate in the teachings of the Prophet Muhammad. Sufi meditation technique has the capacity to contain the direct experiential gnosis of God and then passed on from teacher to student through the centuries. According to Naqshbandi Path, there are six foundations such as: Repetition of Divine Name (Zikr), Meditation (Murakebe), Heart Consciousness, Keeping Contact, Bond of Love and Conversation with the Sheikh (Sohbet).

Bond of Love consists of the affection that unites the seeker to his master. If this state does not arise, the seeker can gain no benefit from his guide; but there is more than this to be discovered.

On the Naqshabandi path, the bond is of four kinds:
1. The seeker pictures in his heart, the face of his master and annihilates himself in it. As the lover sees the face of his beloved in his own face and loses himself in it, so does the seeker look upon his master. Through the bond they made, he takes on the very being of his master. The seeker's soul is lighted up and shines with the light of his master. If the seeker perseveres in this way, in a short time he becomes a perfected man like his sheikh.

2. He fixes his attention lovingly upon the spirituality of his master. He ascribes so exalted a rank to him that he separates him from the rest of creation. At this moment, the spirituality of the master manifests within the seeker. It raises the seeker above the creation. Slowly, slowly the seeker begins to acquire the state of the sheikh.
3. The seeker represents, in his mind's eye, the spirituality of his guide as a circle of light and pictures himself at the centre of that circle. Such an ecstasy takes possession of him that he goes out of himself. At that moment, the spirituality of his sheikh is reflected in the light of the heart. From this reflection, a light appears in the heart of the seeker and draws him on towards perfection.
4. The seeker seats himself as though he were in the presence of his master. He brings an image of his master before his eyes. But here the seeker must know that the spirituality of the master never separates from his image and whenever and wherever he calls on it, that spiritual image will help him. If the seeker, coming into the presence of the master, annihilates his own self-hood and binds himself to that presence, the master can, in a single instant, raise him to the degree of Illumination.

Yoga Nidra

It is a state of conscious deep sleep. During the practice of Yoga Nidra, the person appears to be sleep, but the consciousness is functioning at a deeper level of awareness. It is sleep with a trace of deep awareness. It is a state of mind in between wakefulness and dream. Normally when we sleep, we lose track of our self and cannot utilize this capacity of the mind. Yoga Nidra enables the person to be conscious in this state and nurture the seed of great will power, inspire the higher self and enjoy the vitality of life.

Although it finds mention in old *tantric* texts, Yoga Nidra was rediscovered 20-odd years ago by Swami Satyananda Saraswati, founder of the Bihar School of Yoga

(BSY) in Munger, eastern India. He translates *Yoga Nidra* as psychic sleep and describes it as a systematic method of inducing complete physical, mental and emotional relaxation, while maintaining awareness at the deeper levels.

Indeed, the practice is so relaxing that it becomes almost impossible to remain awake. But you come out, feeling more rested than you do after a good night's sleep and injected with large doses of energy to tackle the day's tasks. The Swami says that prolonged suspension between wakefulness and sleep — called the hypnogogic state — in *Yoga Nidra* may have untold benefits that go beyond the therapeutic.

In Yoga Nidra, we consciously take our attention to different parts of the body, which activates the nerves in those areas and helps to integrate the impact of the asanas (yoga postures) into our system.

Here is a step-by-step guide to do Yoga Nidra.

Tip: It is a good idea to cover yourself with a blanket to keep yourself warm. The body becomes warm while doing postures and a sudden drop in temperature is not suitable.

1. Lie down straight on your back in Corpse Pose (Shavasana). Close your eyes and relax. Take a few deep breaths in and out. Remember to take slow and relaxed breaths and not ujjayi breaths. Tip: If you feel any discomfort or pain in lower back, adjust your posture or use a pillow to elevate the legs a little for more comfort.
2. Start by gently taking your attention to your right foot. Keep your attention there for a few seconds, while relaxing your foot. Then gently move your attention up to the right knee, right thigh and hip (again, for a couple of seconds). Become aware of your whole right leg. Repeat this process for the left leg.
3. Similarly, take your attention to all parts of the body: genital area, stomach, navel region, chest, right shoulder and right arm, followed by the left shoulder and left arm, throat, face and the top of the head.

4. Take a deep breath in, observe the sensations in your body and relax in this still state for a few minutes.
5. Now, slowly becoming aware of your body and surroundings, turn to your right side and keep lying down for a few more minutes.
6. Taking your own time, you may then slowly sit up and whenever you feel comfortable, slowly and gradually open your eyes.

Coherence Meditation

1. Heart's Changing Rhythm

The heart at rest was once thought to operate much like a metronome, faithfully beating out a regular, steady rhythm. Scientists and physicians now know, however, that this is far from the case. Rather than being monotonously regular, the rhythm of a healthy heart — even under resting conditions — is actually surprisingly *irregular*, with the time interval between consecutive heartbeats constantly changing. This naturally occurring beat-to-beat variation in heart rate is called *heart rate variability (HRV)*.

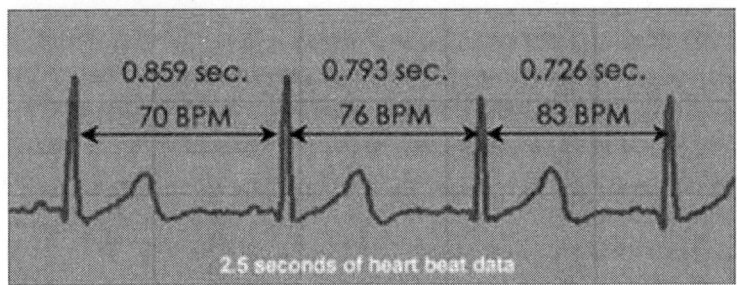

Heart rate variability is a measure of the beat-to-beat changes in heart rate. This diagram shows three heartbeats recorded on an electrocardiogram (ECG). Note that variation in the time interval between consecutive heartbeats. This gives a different heart rate (in beats per minute) for each inter beat interval.

The normal variability in the heart rate is due to the synergistic action of the two branches of the Autonomic Nervous System (ANS), the part of the nervous system that regulates most of the body's internal functions. The sympathetic nerves act to accelerate heart rate, while the parasympathetic (vagus) nerves slow it down. The sympathetic and parasympathetic branches of the ANS are continually interacting to maintain cardiovascular activity in its optimal range and to permit appropriate reactions to changing external and internal conditions. The analysis of HRV, therefore, serves as a dynamic window into the function and balance of the autonomic nervous system.

The moment-to-moment variations in heart rate are generally overlooked when *average* heart rate is measured (for example, when your doctor takes your pulse over a certain period of time and calculates that your heart is beating at, say, 70 beats per minute). However, the Em Wave PC technology allows you to observe your heart's changing rhythms in real time. Using your pulse data, it provides a picture of your HRV, plotting the natural increases and decreases in your heart rate occurring on a continual basis. Physical exercise and even our thoughts affect the breathing and heart rate.

2. Research at the Institute of HeartMath

Research has shown that one of the most powerful factors that affect our heart's changing rhythm is our *feelings and emotions*. When our varying heart rate is plotted over time, the overall shape of the waveform produced is called the heart rhythm pattern. When you use the Em Wave PC, you are seeing your heart rhythm pattern in real time. HeartMath research has found that the emotions we experience directly affect our *heart rhythm pattern* — and this, in turn, tells us much about how our body is functioning.

In general, emotional stress, including emotions such as anger, frustration, and anxiety, gives rise to heart rhythm patterns that appear irregular and erratic. The HRV

Appendix 2

waveform looks like a series of uneven, jagged peaks (an example is shown in the figure below). Scientists call this an *incoherent* heart rhythm pattern. Physiologically, this pattern indicates that the signals produced by the two branches of the ANS are out of sync with each other. This can be likened to driving a car with one foot on the gas pedal (the sympathetic nervous system) and the other on the brake (the parasympathetic nervous system) at the same time—this creates a jerky ride, burns more gas and isn't great for your car, either! Likewise, the incoherent patterns of physiological activity associated with stressful emotions can cause our body to operate inefficiently, deplete our energy and produce extra wear and tear on our whole system. This is especially true if stress and negative emotions are prolonged or experienced often.

In contrast, positive emotions send a very different signal throughout our body. When we experience uplifting emotions such as appreciation, joy, care, and love, our heart rhythm pattern becomes highly ordered, looking like a smooth, harmonious wave (an example is shown in the figure). This is called a *coherent* heart rhythm pattern. When we are generating a coherent heart rhythm, the activity in the two branches of the ANS is synchronized and the body's systems operate with increased efficiency and harmony. It's no wonder that positive emotions feel so good—they actually help our body's systems synchronize and work better.

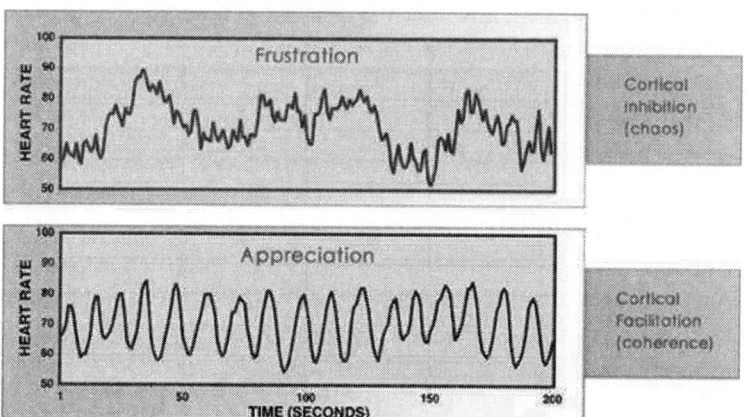

3. Heart rhythm patterns during different emotional states

The graphs given show examples of real-time heart rate variability patterns (heart rhythms) recorded from individuals experiencing different emotions. The *incoherent* heart rhythm pattern shown in the top graph, characterized by its irregular, jagged waveform, is typical of stress and negative emotions such as anger, frustration, and anxiety. The bottom graph shows an example of the *coherent* heart rhythm pattern that is typically observed when an individual is experiencing a sustained positive emotion, such as appreciation, compassion, or love. The coherent pattern is characterized by its regular, sine-wave-like waveform. It is interesting to note that the overall *amount* of heart rate variability is actually the same in the two recordings shown above; however, the *patterns* of the HRV waveforms are clearly different.

4. The Role of breathing

Another important distinction involves understanding the role of breathing in the generation of coherence and its relationship to the techniques of the HeartMath System. Because breathing patterns modulate the heart's rhythm, it is possible to generate a coherent heart rhythm simply by breathing slowly and regularly at a 10-second rhythm (5 seconds on the in-breath and 5 seconds on the out-breath). Breathing rhythmically in this fashion can thus be a useful intervention to initiate a shift out of stressful emotional state and into increased coherence. However, this type of cognitively-directed paced breathing can require considerable mental effort and is difficult for some people to maintain.

5. Emotional shift

While HeartMath techniques incorporate a breathing element, paced breathing is not their primary focus and they should therefore not be thought of simply as breathing exercises.

Appendix 2

The main difference between the HeartMath tools and most commonly practised breathing techniques is the HeartMath tools' focus on the intentional generation of a heartfelt positive emotional state. This *emotional shift* is a key element of the techniques' effectiveness. Positive emotions appear to excite the system at its natural resonant frequency and thus enable coherence to emerge and to be maintained naturally, without conscious mental focus on the person's breathing rhythm. This is because the input generated by the heart's rhythmic activity is actually one of the main factors that affect our breathing rate and patterns. When the heart's rhythm shifts into coherence as a result of a positive emotional shift, our breathing rhythm automatically synchronizes with the heart, thereby reinforcing and stabilizing the shift to system-wide coherence.

www.heartmath.org
www.coherence.com

Glossary and Explanatory Notes

- *Adi Shankaracharya:* Early 8th century philosopher and theologian from India who consolidated the doctrine of Advaita Vedanta. He is credited with unifying and establishing the main currents of thought in Hinduism. His works in Sanskrit discuss the unity of the ātman and Nirguna Brahman or "Brahman without attributes". He wrote copious commentaries on Brahma Sutras, Principal Upanishads and Bhagavad Gita. He also set up four centres (Maths) of learning at Badrinath in north, Dwarka in west, Jagannath Puri in east and Sringeri in south of India.
- *Aham Brahmasmi:* I am the Truth. Assertion that, as Atman, the Jivatma is one with Paramatma.
- *Ahankar:* The "*I*"-sense or ego-sense or "*I*"-consciousness which appropriates all experience to our self.
- *Arjun:* A Pandava, excelling in archery, to whom Bhagavad Gita is addressed.
- *Artha:* Purusartha to acquire wealth, resources.
- *Asanas:* Third step to Yoga (suitable posture).
- *Ashtang yoga:* Eight steps of yoga, propounded by an ancient seer.
- *Atman:* Spirit; Life; Consciousness; Self; that all pervasive consciousness (Paramatma) which is the "Life" within each living being (Jivatma).
- *Beads:* Used in *maala* or garland, to keep count during prayers.

Glossary and Explanatory Notes 159

- *Bhagavad Gita:* Essence of Vedanta.
- *Buddhi:* The decision-making faculty of mind.
- *Chitta:* The stuff of mind where all impressions, memory is retained.
- *Coherent breathing:* Breathing in which heart rate synchronizes with respiration, developed by Stephen Elliott.
  www.coherence.com , and www.heartmath.org.
- *Dharana:* Sixth step to Yoga; fixing the mind on (holy) object of contemplation.
- *Dharma:* That which supports the inherent nature of a thing, e.g., "dharma" of sugar is to give sweetness; moral ethical conduct; dharma supports experiencing of *ananda* or bliss; the inherent nature of a living-being; the critical path of righteous conduct/kartavya-palan to achieve highest Perfection; first purushartha.
- *Dhyan:* Seventh step to Yoga; ability to hold mind on object of contemplation.
- *Drig Dishya Vivek:* A book written by H. H. Adi Shankaracharaya explaining discrimination between the observer and observed.
- *Freeze-Frame:* An instrument used by Heartmath Institute to record and analyse the heart rate variation
- *Gate shoko na kartavyo, bhavishyam na chintayet; Vartman kalen vilakshanam*: It is not our duty to worry about the past or have anxiety about the future; the time is defined by the present moment
- *Gurukul:* A traditional system of education in ancient India.
- *Kaam:* Purusartha to fulfil desires.
- *Kshamavani parva:* A festival of Jains for forgiveness.
- *Magna*: Fully involved in an activity.
- *Mantras:* A holy name or brief prayer used for chanting.
- *Meditation:* Dhyana, mind remains like an un-flickering flame of a candle in a windless place.

- *Moksha:* Freedom from all duality; highest human Perfection; realizing our oneness with God; realizing a state of perpetual peace and bliss.
- *Nirvana:* Highest Perfection.
- *Niyama:* Second step to Yoga; cultivation of good habits.
- *Non-dual Brahman:* The One God; God alone is there.
- *Pooja rituals:* Holy ceremonies to purify the mind by keeping it focused on God.
- *Pranayama:* Fourth step to Yoga; rhythmic breathing.
- *Pratyahar:* Fifth step to Yoga; withdrawing mind from sense-objects.
- *Purushartha:* Four human strivings namely dharma, artha, kaam and moksha.
- *Rajasik:* Passion, prejudice and the resultant activities. The average or human quality of mind.
- *Saattvik:* Represents light, wisdom and happiness The highest quality of mind.
- *Sadhana:* Striving for realizing the (highest) goal.
- *Samadhi:* Eighth (final) step to Yoga; when mind merges totally in object of contemplation.
- *Satsang:* Keeping company with Truth; where highest truth are discussed)
- *Sidhhi:* Supernatural powers that accrue through Yoga.
- *Tamasik:* A deterrent which produces ignorance, delusion, lethargy and sleep; the lowest quality of mind.
- *Transcendental Meditation technique:* Popularized by Mahesh Yogi in the 1970s.
- *Upanishad:* The knowledge portion of the Vedas containing its essence.
- *Yama:* First step to Yoga; Restraining harmful urges of mind.
- *Yoga:* Methods to realize the highest Truth.
- *Yoga Nidra:* Visualization.

References

Balavhandran, Bala V. and A. Kavipriya, *Living legends, learning lessons up close and personal with 10 global icons*, Westland Ltd., 2015

Bodhananda, Swami, *The Gita & Management*, Bluejay Books, 1994

Brantley, Jaffrey, *Calming your anxious mind*, New Harbinger Publications, 2007

Chandar, K. Suresh, *Inspiring Saint*, Sri Vidya Foundation, Madras, 1995

Chung Tsai Chih, *Zen Speaks*, Harper Collins, 1994

Covey, Stephen R., *First thing First*, Simon & Schuster, UK, 1995

Covey, Stephen R., *The Seven Habits of Highly Effective People*, Simon & Schuster, UK, 1989

Csikszentmihalyi Mihaly, *Flow: The Psychology of Happiness*, Harper and Row, 1992

Dalai Lama, His Holiness and Howard C. Cutter, *The Art of Happiness*, Coronet Books, 1998

Dayananda, Swami, *The Teaching of the Bhagwat Gita*, Vision Books Pvt. Ltd., 1989

Dwoskin, Hale, *The Sedona Method*, Sedona Press, 2003

Eliott, Steve, The New Science of Breath

Hanh, Thich Nhat, *Buddha: Knowing the better way to live alone* (ref. The Sutra on knowing the better way to live alone—Badder karatta Sutra), Translated, in his book "Our appointment with life", Parallax Press, Berkley, California, 1990

Hanh, Thich Nhat, *Our Appointment with Life, The Budha's Teaching on Living in the Present*, Parallax Press Berkley, California

Hart, William, *The Art of Living, Vipassana Meditation*, Vipassana Research Institute, Igatpuri, Maharashtra

Khalsa, Dr. Dharam Singh, *Meditation and Medicine*
Krishnamurti, J., *Meditations*, Krishnamurti Foundation India, 1979
Lieber, Nancy, and Sandra Moss, *Healing Depression The Mind Body Way – Creating Happiness With Meditation, Yoga And Ayurveda*, Wiley India
Mahapragya, Acharya, *Truth of Life*, Pathfinder Trust, Sterling Publishers, New Delhi, 2001
Osborne Arthur, *The Teachings of Sri Ramana Maharshi*, Sri Ramasramam Trivannmalai, 1977
Palhan, R. K., *Yoga without sweat and stress*
Palladino PhD, Lucy, *Find your focus zone*, Free Press, 2007
Paramananda, Swami Bharati................
Parthasarathy A., *Atmabodha: Knowledge of self*, Vedanta Life Institute, Bombay
Rama Swami, *Meditation and its Practice*, Himalayan Institute Press, Honesdale, Pennsylvania
Saaraswati, Swami Anubhavananda, *Guided Meditation*
Schrieder, David Servan, *The Secret Teachings*
Seaward, Brian Luke, *Quite Mind Fearless Heart–The Taoist Path Through Stress And Spirituality*, Wiley India, 2010
Sivananda Swami, *Concentration and Meditation*, Divine Life Society Publication, 11th edition, 2005
Sivananda, Swami, *Japa Yoga*, Divine Life Publication, 2005
Sivananda, Swami, *Mind, its mysteries and control*, Divine Life Society Publication, Sat Bhawana Trust, Mumbai,1999
Sivananda, Swami, *Ten Upanishads*, Divine Life Society Publication, 1993
Someswarananda, Swami, *Indian Wisdom for Management*, Ahmedabad Management Association, 1996
Sri Sharada Peetham, *Golden Words of the Glorious Gurus*, 1995
Tatishwarananda, Swami, *Meditation and Spiritual Life*, Ramakrishna Math Bangalore, 5th edition, 1995
Tolle, Eckhart, *Stillness Speaks*, Yogi Impression Books Pvt. Ltd., 2003
Tolle, Eckhart, *The Power of Now*, Yogi Impression Books Pvt., Ltd.
Walsch, Neale Donald, The only thing that matters, Hay House India, 2013

Anxiety